A Culturally Proficient

Society

Begins in School

Jessie,

I appreciate the support and friendship you gave me as I wrote my story.

For all the children,

Love, Carmella

12-11-11

Dedicated to my late father Al Padilla, my mother Margaret Lara Padilla,
and my paternal grandmother Teresa Torres Padilla
for setting the stage that ultimately led to the writing of "my story."
—Carmella Franco

Because they modeled courage and the importance of family,
this book is dedicated to my parents,
my late father Alfred Gutierrez and my mother Anni Gutierrez.
—Maria Ott

This book is dedicated to two women who have taught me the importance of family through
their actions, strength, courage, and unconditional love—
my mother Mary O. Parra, who continues to inspire me every day, and
my maternal grandmother Refugio Ocampo.
—Darline Robles

A Culturally Proficient Society Begins in School

LEADERSHIP *for* EQUITY

Carmella S. Franco
Maria G. Ott
Darline P. Robles

FEATURING CONVERSATIONS WITH

Randall B. Lindsey *and*
Stephanie M. Graham

FOREWORD BY

Thelma Meléndez de Santa Ana

CORWIN
A SAGE Company

CORWIN
A SAGE Company

FOR INFORMATION:

Corwin

A SAGE Company

2455 Teller Road

Thousand Oaks, California 91320

(800) 233-9936

Fax: (800) 417-2466

www.corwin.com

SAGE Ltd.

1 Oliver's Yard

55 City Road

London EC1Y 1SP

United Kingdom

SAGE India Pvt. Ltd.

B 1/I 1 Mohan Cooperative Industrial Area

Mathura Road, New Delhi 110 044

India

SAGE Asia-Pacific Pte. Ltd.

33 Pekin Street #02-01

Far East Square

Singapore 048763

Acquisitions Editor: Dan Alpert

Associate Editor: Megan Bedell

Editorial Assistant: Sarah Bartlett

Production Editors: Cassandra Margaret
Seibel and
Veronica Stapleton

Copy Editor: Codi Bowman

Typesetter: C&M Digitals (P) Ltd.

Proofreader: Dennis W. Webb

Indexer: Sheila Bodell

Cover Designer: Scott Van Atta

Permissions Editor: Karen Ehrmann

Copyright © 2011 by Corwin

Printed in the United States of America

Library of Congress Cataloging-in-Publication Data

Franco, Carmella S.

A culturally proficient society begins in school : leadership for equity / Carmella S. Franco, Maria G. Ott & Darline P. Robles; featuring conversations with Randall B. Lindsey & Stephanie M. Graham; foreword by Thelma Meléndez de Santa Ana.

p. cm.
Includes bibliographical references and index.

ISBN 978-1-4129-8653-3 (pbk.)

1. School management and organization—Social aspects—United States. 2. Multicultural education—United States. 3. Educational equalization—United States. 4. School improvement programs—United States. I. Ott, Maria G. II. Robles, Darline P. III. Lindsey, Randall B. IV. Graham, Stephanie M. V. Title.

LB2805.F665 2011
371.2′07—dc23   2011019159

This book is printed on acid-free paper.

11 12 13 14 15 10 9 8 7 6 5 4 3 2 1

Contents

Foreword

America's growing diverse society has an increasing need for educators who appreciate the nation's cultural heritages. The nation's minorities in aggregate have become the majority population in our public schools, and as they grow up the United States will become a minority majority nation. If we are to meet these, our students' needs, it is imperative that we acknowledge and capitalize on the assets of their rich cultural heritages.

In this book, Carmella Franco, Maria Ott, and Darline Robles share the experiences that molded them into successful school superintendents. They share their inspirational stories of braving discrimination, of incorporating their cultural values into the profession, and—without forgetting the classroom child—of maximizing each opportunity to be the best candidate for the next job.

With authentic voices they reveal their personal experiences as leaders in a system that still has not fully opened its doors of opportunity to all students. The authors speak frankly about the problems they faced as educational leaders of color, and as women in charge of male-dominated institutions. Structuring their contributions as personal journals, the authors discuss how they dealt successfully with intransigent school district trustees, unsupportive supervisors and co-workers, and all the other obstacles that our discriminatory society set in their way.

Equally important, they vigorously affirm that their home cultures have enriched them as individuals and contributed to their professional success. They drew on deep wells of community support, effectively tackled ingrained institutional problems with culturally guided strategies, and lent their strong voices to students and families who previously had no one in a position of power to speak for them.

These three women tore down public educational barriers, creating effective programs to address student needs to bring greater acceptance of different cultures to classrooms, thereby enlarging the experiences of all their students.

As a Latina who has also served as an urban school district superintendent and in a national leadership position, I recognize first hand the challenges that these authors faced. I also can personally vouch for the challenges that so many Latino and other language minority children continue to experience in our public schools. Their stories are real; they are achingly honest.

While each woman speaks about her unique experience as a successful educational professional, the theme of home culture weaves through each narrative. At one time, this nation blatantly repressed its cultural and gender differences. Now our somewhat wiser country more readily acknowledges that these differences will not fragment us, but will make us a stronger and more enlightened people. By embracing our differences, we can face the challenges of the 21st century with more confidence.

The authors acknowledge the mentors who helped them navigate their career paths at a time when there were no Latina role models. Now, they mentor a new generation of aspiring superintendents. I too have asked advice of each of these wise women at one time or another. I can confirm that they speak authoritatively about the assets that a strong Latina leader can bring to public education.

Our culture helps to define our identity. To understand one's home culture is an essential for a self-examined life. This book may compel you to examine your own core values. Like the authors themselves, their book can be a change agent: as it retraces each author's life path, it poses core questions that all of us should address.

The book will ask you to consider your personal relationship to your own culture. How has your own family culture affected your outlook and fundamental beliefs? What aspects of your home culture do you still live by, and what have you left behind? How do you reconcile home values and majoritarian values? How do you respond to societal change? How well do you embrace the values of other cultures? And how do you—as a public sector professional—cope with individuals and organizations that subtly or deliberately denigrate certain groups of children, or their parents and communities?

Their book can prompt you to consider your own life narrative, and to acknowledge the cultures around you and those of your own heritage. As you read the chapters detailing the steps each of these remarkable women took to build her career, you will be asked to respond to the same questions they addressed at crucial points in their career, and to take a deeper look into yourself.

This book is more than a trilogy of memoirs, a career-building guide, or a much-needed look into the impact of culture and education. It is a thought-provoking exercise that we all can carry out to better understand ourselves, our nation's cultures, and the importance of keeping an open heart and mind to the differences that children bring to the public schoolhouse door. Their narratives can help us give proper perspective to the children's cultural treasures, which in turn can help us sustain our nation's preeminence in the new century.

Thelma Meléndez de Santa Ana, PhD
Assistant Secretary for Elementary and Secondary Education
U.S. Department of Education

Acknowledgments

We are grateful for the many people who have contributed to the completion of this book, the patient support and sacrifices of our families, the contributions of professional colleagues, and the inspiration of friends. Our words here are to honor their support for this work.

No story is complete without a listing of the main characters. I, Carmella Franco, wish to thank those individuals who continue and/or have continued to play a role in my life and career. They include my husband Tom Jackson, who has been rooting for me throughout most of my administrative career, and without whose encouragement and belief, I would not be where I am today; and my family members who have been there in the rafters as I moved through the different positions in education, and continue to support me in my current role as State Trustee. My husband, family, and, also, dear friends share in the joy of my realizing a longtime dream of writing a book centered on women making a difference in educational administration. Additionally, I must acknowledge past mentors who believed in me and cheered me on in my pursuits, especially University of La Verne Doctoral Program Cluster Leader Dr. Patricia Clark White, along with former board member John L. Peel, who was a true champion of my efforts to improve educational opportunities for students in Whittier City School District, where I served as Superintendent for 12 years. I am indebted to these individuals, and to so many more, who have been important in my life.

I, Maria Ott, especially thank my husband Thomas Ott for being my anchor and support while raising our two children and advancing my career. He always offered words of encouragement when I had doubts about being a mother and a professional. Our marriage of 41 years is a gift that I cherish. My children Kathryn Ott Carey and Thomas Ott have wonderful spouses, and they have blessed me with five beautiful granddaughters. I also appreciate two powerful mentors, and I am grateful for their guidance. I especially thank Amelia McKenna, who was both supervisor and friend during my years working in bilingual leadership roles for the Los Angeles Unified School District. She is an amazing woman who was never afraid to challenge the institutional impediments that denied educational equity to children who were not native speakers of English. Her friendship has helped me during many difficult decisions in my life and career. I also thank my coauthor Darline Robles for pushing me when I needed extra encouragement to take on new career opportunities. Her wisdom was invaluable, and her friendship is cherished. Finally, I have benefited from many colleagues, both male and female, who have supported me during my career. I value my professional relationships and hope that this book will serve as a tribute to the gifted educators who have touched my life and helped shape my belief that courage, compassion, and commitment are essential to leadership.

I, Darline Robles, could not be where I am today without the love and support of my husband Frank. He has been with me through many days and nights when I thought I could not go on—through his encouragement, I was able to achieve many of my aspirations. To my son Lawrence, for his patience and understanding while I was moving up the career ladder. To my granddaughter Lauren, the joy of our lives, who continues to teach me every day about the wonder of childhood and keeps me grounded in what truly matters in life. And to my brother Lorenzo, who has been with me longer than anyone, other than my mother, for his love, and most of all for always cheering me on to be the best I can be. To my father, who passed away too young, but pushed me hard to reach my goals; I know he is pleased with what I have accomplished. And to all my family and friends, I wish I could name all of you, but you know who you are—thank you for always being there for me! I would be remiss if I didn't mention two mentors, who early on saw something in me, as a young teacher, and gave me the skills and support to advance in my career on behalf of children: Nicholas Mansour, my first principal, whom I admire to this day for his unwavering love and support of all students. His willingness to do whatever it took to save students' lives and to inspire his staff to do the same is why I decided to become an administrator. Thanks also go to Dr. Mary Gonzales Mend, my friend. Mary, the first Latina principal in Montebello USD was a role model for me and is a person I am grateful to call my mentor and friend. Without her continued support and encouragement, I would never have taken on the challenge of becoming a superintendent. Both Nick and Mary embody the leadership qualities of uncompromising commitment to all children and the ability to inspire others to be the best they can be; thank you both for being my role models. And to so many others who have been part of my professional life, I continue to learn from you and will always be thankful to you for allowing me to be part of your lives. I hope you will find in this book the lessons I learned from so many of you, as we all continue our work to make a difference in children's lives.

We three coauthors are extremely grateful to Randall B. Lindsey for his guidance and direction during the writing of the book, and to Stephanie Graham for her guidance in the construction of the book's rubric. A special thank you to Delores B. Lindsey for her careful review and editing of our manuscript.

We learned about Corwin from our colleagues, Randy and Stephanie, and cannot imagine having a more supportive publisher. Dan Alpert, our acquisitions editor, has been our advocate for telling our stories and embodies the commitment to social justice that we have come to associate with Corwin. Appreciation goes to Megan Bedell, Associate Editor, and Sarah Bartlett, Senior Editorial Assistant, who are carefully guiding us through the process of making our work a reality.

About the Authors

Carmella S. Franco, EdD, is a State Trustee, appointed by the California State Board of Education to oversee the academically failing Alisal Union Elementary School District in Monterey County. After retiring from 12 years as Superintendent of the Whittier City School District in 2008, Carmella then served for nearly one year as an Interim Superintendent of the Woodland Joint Unified School District. Her 38 years in public education include having served as director of personnel, elementary and middle school principal, English as a second language (ESL) specialist and Title VII director in diverse school district settings, all with high English language learner student populations. Carmella's passion is in ensuring that students of color are provided with every opportunity to succeed, in particular, with access to higher education. She often copresents on women in educational leadership roles, and currently, she directs the Association of California School Administrator's Superintendents Academy in Whittier, California.

Dr. Franco received her EdD in 1991 from the University of LaVerne.

Maria G. Ott, PhD, continues as the superintendent of the award-winning Rowland (CA) Unified School District where she has led educational transformation efforts for six years. Prior to being recruited to Rowland Unified, she served five years as the senior deputy superintendent to Roy Romer in the Los Angeles Unified School District, supervising major reform efforts. She was recruited by Roy Romer, a nontraditional superintendent and the former three-term Governor of Colorado, to serve as his educational deputy following seven successful years as superintendent of the

Little Lake City School District where she raised student achievement and received national recognition for her leadership. Prior to becoming superintendent of Little Lake City Schools in 1993, Maria Gutierrez Ott was a teacher, site administrator, and central office administrator in the Los Angeles Unified School District, recognized for her instructional leadership and her work to improve the performance of English learners. Maria Gutierrez Ott earned her PhD from the University of Southern California.

 **Darline P. Robles, PhD,** is currently a Professor of Clinical Education at the Rossier School of Education, University of Southern California. Her primary responsibility as professor is the development of a new national hybrid (online and on-campus) master's degree program in school leadership. Her duties also include teaching and supervising graduate students and providing service to the School, the University, and the larger professional community.

Dr. Robles recently retired as the superintendent of the Los Angeles County Office of Education, where she served eight years. As the top education leader of the nation's most populous and diverse county, she ensured the financial and academic stability of 80 school districts that serve more than two million preschool and school-aged children. She was the first woman to be named superintendent of the Los Angeles County Office of Education (LACOE). In 2002, Dr. Robles oversaw $16 billion in school district funding and a staff of nearly 4,000.

Closing the achievement gap is Dr. Robles's highest priority. She is acclaimed as a state leader in implementing the Williams legislation, a landmark law enacted in 2004 to promote educational equity through monitoring of 600 low-performing schools annually to ensure that all students have access to textbooks, safe and clean facilities, and qualified teachers.

Dr. Robles has also attained unprecedented success in organizing superintendents and forging partnerships with local, state, and national officials to promote policies and programs that advance educational opportunities for underserved student groups. In addition, she has dedicated a record level of human and financial resources to improving services provided to the thousands of at-risk and special-needs students enrolled in LACOE-run schools.

As chief of the Salt Lake City School District from 1995 to 2002, Dr. Robles was recognized for raising student achievement, significantly reducing the dropout rate, and securing vital resources for needy schools. Such efforts include obtaining a $12 million Annenberg

Challenge Grant to support district-wide reform and spearheading a $136 million capital bond measure that gained the support of nearly 75 percent of voters.

Earlier, as Superintendent of the Montebello Unified School District, she saved that district from a state takeover by returning it to financial stability within two years. The California native formally began her 30-year education career in Montebello as a teacher, then coordinator, of bilingual and bicultural education and also served as an elementary and intermediate school principal.

Dr. Robles received her bachelor of arts degree in history from California State University, Los Angeles; her master's degree in education from Claremont Graduate School; and her doctorate in education policy and administration from the University of Southern California.

In October 2009, she was named one of the Top 100 Influential Hispanic Americans by *Hispanic Business Magazine,* and in March 2010 she was a "Women of the Year" recipient of the L.A. County Commission for Women. Dr. Robles is committed to public service and serves on many local and national boards. She was recently named to the President's Advisory Commission on Educational Excellence for Hispanics.

She is married and has one son and one granddaughter. The Robleses live in Whittier.

Randall B. Lindsey is principal associate of The Robins Group. He is professor emeritus at California State University, Los Angeles, where he served as chair of the Division of Administration and Counseling in the School of Education. He has served as a junior and senior high school teacher of history and as an administrator of school desegregation and staff development programs. He has worked extensively with school districts as they plan for and experience changing populations.

Stephanie M. Graham is principal associate of Educational Equity Solutions. She develops and implements training programs for teachers, administrators, and other support staff to help them understand and dismantle the various barriers to student access, opportunities, and success. She has been a teacher and administrator at the secondary and university level, and has developed and managed local, regional, and state programs focusing on educational equity. Stephanie's many honors include recognition by One America in the 21st Century—President Clinton's initiative on race relations. Stephanie is also a coauthor of *Culturally Proficient Inquiry: A Lens for Examining Education Gaps,* published by Corwin.

Introduction

Our Purpose in Writing This Book

It is our belief that all educational leaders, male and female from all cultural groups, have the capacity to be successful when they have an understanding of the importance of students' cultures being viewed and treated as an asset. We are sharing our stories and our lessons of progress and success to inform the practices of current and future leaders and policy makers. It is our observation that the United States and Canada are at a tipping point in their ability and willingness to address the needs of historically and currently underserved groups. However, the barriers to progress are so deeply entrenched in social institutions, such as education, that we must realize educational and social reforms are inextricably interlinked.

Recently, education in the United States and Canada has expanded so that educators are being challenged and have the opportunity to provide high-quality education to all children and youth. Students from historically underserved populations are arriving in our schools in ever-growing numbers, and educators are expected to provide them with the same quality of education that was reserved for middle- and upper-class students even 40 years ago. Today's schools are being challenged to expand the quality of education provided historically to well-served populations in a manner that inclusively values formerly marginalized gender, racial, ethnic, English learning, and special needs cultures. As superintendents, our mission is to lead socioculturally diverse schools in serving students in an equitable manner.

Linking Equity and Inclusivity

Our professional careers began in the early 1970s and have evolved to demonstrate how educational equity is fostered and achieved in our society. The social and cultural dynamics of preceding generations impacted our careers by providing barriers and enhancements that affected our successes as educational leaders. The social dynamics of exclusion of women and people of color from the mainstream of society are coupled, for us, with the cultural dynamics of growing up Latina in the United States. In preparing this manuscript, we identified dynamics that served as barriers to our progress; whereas, other dynamics served as support systems for our successes. What has been clear to us is that barriers to progress have not been isolated incidents; rather, they have been deeply rooted systemic forces that impact nondominant groups throughout society, not just in education. We found that recognizing barriers to education is an important step in creating educational equity that enhances the education of all students in our schools.

Through sharing our stories with you, you will come to know us as fairly typical educators of our generation who were reared in supportive families, were successful in school, and who became teachers intent on helping all students succeed to their highest potential. You also will learn that we honed our leadership interests early in life and had educational and real-life experiences that made us aware of the context in which we were living. The social and political context of this country in the latter 20th century and the second decade of the 21st century have influenced our leadership philosophies and our dedication to equitable educational opportunities for all children. We are deeply committed to a democratic society, and we believe that our commitment to all youth and adult learners is in the best interest of our nation.

It would have been easy for us to frame this book by vividly describing the discrimination we have experienced and witnessed in our lives and careers. Make no mistake; those events have occurred, as you will see in the chapters that follow. However, our focus is to share with you how we have used those events as motivation to increase educational opportunities for all children and youth.

Our P–12 education, our early experiences as teachers moving into leadership positions, and our current roles as superintendents have provided us with unique perspectives and experiences. Although we do not purport to represent all Latinas or women-of-color superintendents, we believe our *culturally proficient lessons for being successful in diverse communities* can inform other educators who desire to extend the promises of democracy to all cultural groups who attend our public schools.

This book is written to offer you these perspectives stated as benefits:

- All school leaders will benefit by seeing how the improvement of opportunities for those least well served in our society results in all boats rising.
- All educators as nonformal and formal leaders—administrators, teachers, and counselors—will benefit in learning to recognize and acknowledge barriers to equitable educational opportunities and outcomes to create educational equity.
- Educational leaders in schools/districts where students have been historically well served will benefit by recognizing that high-quality education for some students is inextricably linked to excellence for all students in meeting our mission of preparing well-educated citizens. As we progress into the 21st century, we become a country that is more diverse and potentially more inclusive than at any time in our history.

You are invited to use our journey as described in these chapters to think deeply about your educational journey, not only the one already travelled but also the journey that lies ahead with your school, district, and community.

1

The *Why* of This Book

For all the children.

Moll (2010, p. 451)

We recognize that women of color have much to teach all educators about using leadership to transform schools and society. Most books about educational leadership have been written, either explicitly or implicitly, from a white, male perspective and experience. This book is written from a complementary perspective to add the perspective of women and, in our case, women of color. At the same time, this is a work about how all educators have the social responsibility and professional means to lead in the education of all children, youth, and adult learners. We honor our predecessors and contemporaries, and use this book to build on what we have learned from and with those educators and researchers.

An emerging and energetic reality in our schools and districts serves to shape our views about leadership for education in the 21st century and is best summarized by these statements:

- Few women are school superintendents in the United States. A 2010 study by the American Association of School Administrators found that 24.1% of school superintendents were women (Kowalski, McCord, Petersen, Young, & Ellerson, 2011, p. 18).

- Even fewer school superintendents are women of color (Grogan & Shakeshaft, 2011). Only 6.13% of school superintendents were classified as people of color in 2006 (Glass & Franceschini, 2007, p. 14), and still only 6% in 2010 (Kowalski et al., p. 20).
- Women of color experience unique challenges in leadership roles.
- Women of color bring unique experiences and strengths to school leadership.
- Women of color change schools and society through their leadership roles.
- All educators can benefit collectively from educating all children in our society.
- The student population of our schools is very diverse, as reflected in 2006 data: 56% white, 20% Latino, 17% African American, almost 5% Asian/Pacific Islander, and 2% First Nations and other demographic, cultural groups (Snyder, Dillow, & Hoffman, 2009).
- Nationally, 83% of teachers are white, 8% are black, 6% are Latino, and all other groups comprised 3% (National Center for Education Statistics, 2007; U.S. Department of Education, 2007).

These statements and data not only serve to inform us but also serve to motivate us to recognize that society is ever evolving, and in the 21st century, we cannot be bound by a past that consigned some cultural groups to the margins of society. School leaders in the 21st century must view their roles to guide themselves and fellow educators to identify barriers to student access and achievement by having the will, skill, and ability to recognize and use students' cultural assets as foundations for lifelong learning.

Educational Transformation: The Context and Purpose of This Book

Educational transformation cannot occur in a society that hinders the progress of some of its people either as blindness to their plight or intentional attempts to restrict their access (Fullan, 2003). Educational transformation can only occur when individuals and institutions representing multiple perspectives and experiences stop blaming underserved groups and, instead, embrace the education of underserved students as societal struggles and commit to doing whatever it takes to bring balance to systems where some demographic groups are systematically and disproportionately preempted from opportunities for success. Society requires that schools deliver graduates who are proficient learners and who can competently work in diverse social settings.

This book speaks to all educators in ways that bring us together in a common vision of an education system in which all educators, across the diversity spectrum, assume responsibility and commitment to high-level education for all children, youth, and adult learners. During our lives, our country has experienced social and economic changes that continue to affect our school systems in fundamental ways. Three social changes evolving over the last two generations impact becoming an effective school leader, particularly a superintendent of schools where disparities in achievement have become public issues. These changes are the following:

- It is no longer acceptable to ignore student underachievement. Educational leaders must assume responsibility for narrowing and closing achievement disparities in our schools regarding students who have special needs: students from low-socioeconomic groups, as well as students who are English learners, African Americans, Latinos, First Nations, and Southeast Asian.
- All students must graduate from our secondary schools prepared for college and/or professions and careers of the 21st century. Insulation from economic and technology changes in society serves as an equity challenge, and impedes our ability to educate all students to high levels. Educators who have not been affected by the economic and technology changes may not understand the extent to which the changing job market either has cultivated a need for higher levels of education or has fostered a permanent underclass of people consigned to menial labor jobs.
- School leaders must be able to lead schools in ways that motivate fellow educators to see and achieve equitable outcomes for their students. In doing so, school leaders must possess skills that are both transactional and transformational. Given that most schools are organized in traditional bureaucratic form and function, it is important that school leaders are able to create and work with structures that provide the transactional leadership of clear expectations and guidelines for the work to be done. Transformational leadership focuses on working with others to develop their capacity to lead and to achieve shared goals and vision (Bass & Riggio, 2006).

On the social front, judicial, legislative, and executive mandates have been enacted to lessen or eliminate discrimination and to provide access to cultural groups of people formerly excluded or restricted from full participation in society. While legal avenues were being pursued to expand access to full citizenship for voting and public education, our country was undergoing a tumultuous change from a manufacturing, industrial-based society to an information-based, technologically oriented society. Expanding civil rights and a rapidly changing economy now require educators and, in particular, educational leaders to have an inclusive, culturally proficient vision for our society and to lead schools from which students graduate to be active participants in an ever-changing, evolving society.

Cultural Proficiency Is Transformative

Some of us learn cultural proficiency from reading books such as this one or attending professional development sessions to provoke our thinking and action. Others of us learn cultural proficiency from personal experiences. It is within the purpose of this book to share the lessons for success from the life experiences of three Latina superintendents. These lessons will support you to examine and plan your leadership journey. During this journey, you will enhance your effectiveness with diverse communities by applying the tools of cultural proficiency. In the process, transforming education cannot be a separate enterprise from transforming society. In fact, once you experience using the lens of Cultural Proficiency to examine your values and behaviors and the policies and practices of your school, you will find yourself being mindful of the manner in which barriers impede access to equitable opportunities for cultural groups that exist in our society. More important, you will empower yourself to be an agent for working with others to recognize barriers and to be intentional in providing equitable opportunities for historically underserved students.

Our Lives and Careers Parallel an Increasingly Inclusive United States

As we indicated in the Introduction to this book, it is through sharing our stories with you that you will come to know us as fairly typical educators of our generation who were reared in supportive families, who were successful in school, and who became teachers intent on helping all students succeed to their highest potential. We were born in the late 1940s and early 1950s, and grew up in an era when numerous landmark judicial decisions and legislative acts expanded access to voting, employment, and education. These decisions and cases are particularly poignant for us because many of our parents and other relatives were marginalized in explicit ways that the three of us do not experience today. However, the implicit marginalization too often present in our school systems is what confronts all of us in the second decade of the 21st century.

We summarize the evolving social and political contexts that have served to inform our vision of educational leadership for the 21st century. Each of the judicial decisions and legislative acts described in this section has served to inform the values we have developed for serving historically underserved populations of students. In the end, these judicial decisions and legislative acts have served to create an increase in morally and democratically inclusive nations.

Given your interest in the topic of this book, it is likely that we share a common interest in the historic events that shaped our lives. In fact, on some fronts, much work remains to be done, and after reading this book, if not already involved, you might choose to become an active participant. Whether you are familiar with these events, place yourself in the role of being someone who could be affected directly by these decisions. Implicit to each of the events is a legacy of discrimination; explicit to each event is the promise of a democracy striving to fulfill its promise to all citizens. With the context of the former firmly in our minds, the latter fuels our passion as educational leaders.

We have selected prominent court decisions and legislative acts to illustrate the expanding nature of access to educational opportunity in our country. We fully recognize that we have omitted decisions and acts you might consider as important as those we cited. Our purpose is only to demonstrate the expansion of basic rights, not to provide a comprehensive study of equal educational opportunity, and to note that the work of democracy is not yet finished. In fact, on some fronts, much work remains to be done, and in reading this book, you might choose to become an active participant.

During Our Early Years

While we were in our formative years, two important court decisions were enacted that, unbeknown to us, would shape our personal and professional lives in ways we could not have imagined. These court cases are foundations for our work as school leaders.

Mendez v. Westminster, 1946. This California State Supreme Court decision provided Governor Earl Warren the opportunity to end the legal segregation of Mexican and Mexican American students from white students. An interesting sidelight of this decision is the complainant, the Mendez family, was offered the right to attend the predominately white school in their neighborhood if they would drop the case. Moll (2010) reports the Mendez family recognized the importance of their lawsuit extended to more than just their family, hence the oft-repeated phrase associated with the *Mendez v. Westminster* decision—*for all the children* (Moll, 2010, p. 451). The National Association for the Advancement of Colored People (NAACP) filed a friend of the court brief and Thurgood Marshall led their legal team.

Brown v. Topeka Board of Education, 1954. This U.S. Supreme Court decision reversed the "separate but equal" provisions of a prior U.S. Supreme Court decision, *Plessy v. Ferguson* (1896). Among the acts of discrimination outlawed was school segregation. An interesting note to this decision is that the California *Mendez v. Westminster* (1946) decision provided part of the rationale for striking down *Plessy v. Ferguson*, with former California Governor Earl Warren serving as Chief Justice of the U.S. Supreme Court along with Thurgood Marshall as Justice of the Court.

Our K–12 School Years

During our college years and throughout our early years as teachers, we were well aware of the modern civil rights movement and how inequities were being addressed at the national and local levels. Our careers were intertwined with and strongly influenced by the following legislative acts, court decisions, and emerging acknowledgment of achievement gaps.

1964 Civil Rights Act—Titles IV and VI. This law was crafted and enacted, among other provisions, to end formal segregation in schools against African Americans and women in the United States (Title IV). The law also threatened to remove federal funding (Title VI) from schools where segregation persisted and served to expand the protections of the government to those discriminated against based on their skin color or national origin.

Report of the National Assessment of Educational Progress (NAEP), 1971. In the spring of 1971, NAEP reported and widely disseminated what may be the first documentation of achievement gaps in reading and mathematics among students based on race and gender. NAEP has issued reports yearly since 1971, making seemingly little impact in the educational community in any substantive way that would draw concerted efforts to address the achievement gaps (Perie, Moran, & Lutkus, 2005).

Women's Education Equity Act, 1974. Authorized in Title IV(a) of the 1965 Civil Rights Act, this act provided funds to support Title IX of the Elementary and Secondary Education Amendments of 1972. The program was enacted in 1974 to remedy discrimination against women and girls, including multiple discriminations based on gender, race, ethnicity, national origin, disability, or age. The act has been amended in recent years to address issues of discrimination levied against males.

Lau v. Nichols, 1974. The U.S. Supreme Court, relying on the 14th Amendment to the U.S. Constitution, held that not providing linguistically appropriate educational opportunities was tantamount to national origin discrimination. The decision served as the rationale for expanding bilingual education programs across the country.

Public Law 94-142, Individuals With Disabilities Education Act, 1975. This was enacted to ensure a free and appropriate education for students with disabilities.

Our Years as School Leaders

By the 1990s, we had each served as school principals and district office administrators and were on our way to becoming school superintendents in Salt Lake City and school districts in Los Angeles County. Ultimately, we became superintendent of Los Angeles County Schools, superintendent of the Rowland Unified School District in Los Angeles County, and state-appointed trustee of the Alisal School District in Salinas, California. During our superintendencies, a California Supreme Court decision and Elementary and Secondary School Act (ESEA) Title I legislation helped shape our equity and access agenda for the first decade of the 21st century:

Williams v. California Settlement Case, 2004. This landmark California Supreme Court decision effectively made access to resources an equal opportunity issue. Because of this decision, California school districts are required to provide the necessities of educational opportunity—textbooks and instructional materials, safe and clean schools, and qualified teachers (ACLU of Southern California, 2007, p. 6).

No Child Left Behind (NCLB), 2002 and *Race to the Top, 2009*—The ramifications of these initiatives of the Bush and Obama administrations, respectively, have huge implications for our schools. For our purposes with this book, we highlight that NCLB was the first reauthorization of the ESEA to highlight achievement gaps among students based on race, ethnicity, gender, and social class. Race to the Top is a U.S. Department of Education program funded by the American Reinvestment and Recovery Act intended to spur school reform. Like NCLB, it focuses on closing the achievement gap that persists among ethnic, racial, gender, and social class demographic sectors of our society.

Preparing All Students for the 21st Century

The access to civil and human rights described occurred while Canada and the United States evolved through a blue-collar Industrial Age to a Technology Age. This shift in the economy is having a dramatic impact on society, and it must be reflected by what we do in our schools and classrooms.

During our careers, we have witnessed technology progress from overhead and opaque projectors to rapid technology systems that include high-speed Internet and social media mechanisms. Teachers with today's most basic computer system and access to the Internet can connect themselves and their students to worldwide sources of information not fathomable two generations ago. For our students, not only is the world of information a keystroke away so are future academic and career opportunities. The implication, of course, is that for students to compete in today and tomorrow's career world, they must graduate from high school with an education grounded in solid academic performance and skills that support continuing scholastic and career growth.

The achievement gap first laid bare by the National Assessment of Educational Progress in 1971 was a clarion call to which our educational and political community responded very slowly

(Perie et al., 2005). Our society and our profession have been slow to respond with sustained efforts to narrow or close achievement gaps. The accountability movement of the last decade has described and defined achievement gaps to be more than disproportional in reading and mathematics achievement; achievement gaps also exist in access to technology-based professions and careers. Indeed, the world has changed since we began teaching. At that time, it was possible for a person to receive a few years of high school education, preferably graduate from high school, and gain a job in manufacturing or the trades to provide his family with a middle-class lifestyle. Those choices have evaporated, and unless we want to consign another generation of low-income youth and young adults to menial employment, our schools must approach equity with a renewed sense of urgency. Equity must not mean only providing access based on one's cultural identifier such as race, ethnicity, or gender; equity must also be defined as the quality of education that provides our high school graduates the choice to proceed to university studies or careers in which they can sustain an independent lifestyle.

Equitable Outcomes Are the Goal

Today's schools require leaders who envision what schooling can be for all students, in particular, students from historically marginalized groups, and who marshal human and economic resources for equitable academic outcomes. The first step often entails awareness of disparities correlated with ethnicity, race, gender, and/or social class, and it leads to school staff engaging in needed inquiry about diversity and equity. However, much too often, we experience fellow educators approaching diversity and equity issues as acts of charity. We have witnessed staff development sessions in which the presenter explains that students from designated cultural groups do not have requisite middle-class access to books, newspapers, museums, or other experiences that prepare them for schooling. The expressed or implied message is the students cannot be expected to perform well academically, and the pace of learning has to be slowed to accommodate acquiring requisite middle-class norms that support success in schools. Such forms of charity are in direct conflict with goals of social justice, which moves the locus of responsibility for education of our children to the educators. Our responsibility is to identify students' assets and to remove institutional barriers to the development of those assets in a way that provides students the opportunity to learn at high levels.

Stark contrast exists between these two seemingly similar terms, "charity" and "social justice." Charity and social justice differ in that the former responds with expression and acts of empathy and compassion, whereas the latter addresses the forces that create and foster circumstances of inequity (Rolheiser cited in Conners & Poutiatine, 2010).

Similar stark difference exists between "transactional" and "transformational" leadership. When a leader fixates only on maintaining the status quo and giving little or no substantive attention to lingering issues of inequity, such as disparate student achievement, transactional leadership is at its worst. Transformational leaders understand the need for clarity and a sense of organization in large, complex organizations, such as schools, and pursue a vision that motivates others in the direction of what education *should be.*

As superintendents, we have led schools and school districts to address issues of access and academic achievement disparity. We are witness to schools around the United States and Canada that also hold a vision for equity in classrooms and that view students' culture as an asset on which to build relationships that result in narrowing achievement gaps. Transformation is within the school's organizational culture and the manner in which the school values the ethnic, racial, religious, gender, sexual orientation, ableness, and socioeconomic cultures in the communities they serve.

What Lies Ahead?

Because our lives and careers have experienced societal and economic changes of such a magnitude hardly conceivable two generations ago, we pause and wonder aloud: *What changes are likely ahead for our education systems? In what ways might schools provide for students currently identified as underperforming? Most important, what role do you want to design for yourself and your school to meet the needs of our children, youth, and adult learners?* Please use the space provided to record your thinking.

_____

_____

_____

_____

The Importance of Story

In Chapter 2, you are introduced to our leadership stories. We have taken time to tell our stories to provide you a template for considering and constructing your story. It is in constructing our personal stories and the stories of our schools that we can become intentional in constructing our leadership paradigm and theory of action. Once we know our leadership intent, then we can lead our schools and school districts to understand their histories for purposes of constructing *a new story*. The new story values the diversity within our communities, honors the cultures of our students and their parents, is built on our and our students' assets, recognizes and challenges educator and systemic barriers, and results in student access and achievement.

2

Pueblo, Kronach, and East Los Angeles

Our Beginnings

Women leaders redefine leadership.

Grogan & Shakeshaft (2011, p. 1)

One might rightfully ask, *So where and how did these three successful educational leaders get their start in life?* In this chapter, we begin our stories, so you will know us as people who have grown up in places and with family and community circumstances probably not much different from yours. We want you to know where we were raised, and we want you to know a little about our families.

Carmella Franco's story began in Pueblo, Colorado. Maria Ott's story began in Kronach, Germany. Darline Robles's story began in East Los Angeles, California. As you read this chapter about our earliest years, think about your origins, and at the end of this chapter, we provide you the opportunity to write about your early life. We have designed this book so you can use our stories to understand your story of leadership. We provide writing space for you at the end of each chapter to reflect on and construct your leadership story.

Carmella Franco

During my early years in Pueblo, my parents owned and ran a small mom-and-pop grocery store. We lived in the downstairs apartment of my maternal grandparents' home. All of the extended family, meaning grandparents, great-grandparents, great-great-grandparents, great-aunts and great-uncles, lived within a three-block area. I recall a wonderful time of daily interactions with the family. Pueblo was made up of ethnic neighborhoods. Although Hispanic, we lived in the Italian part of town, and the extended family members spoke fluent Italian. I recall, as a child, entering a room and the language spoken would change from English or Spanish to Italian. My mother's father was fluent in five languages, and my last visit with him prior to his death involved him teaching me basic Italian.

At age five, my mother, father, and younger sister (Christine) boarded a train to Los Angeles. There were two reasons for this permanent move. First, the economy was poor, and second, my father wanted to relocate to be near his parents. My paternal grandparents, who had relocated from near Hillsboro, New Mexico, to California in the mid-1940s, owned three houses on a lot. We moved into the middle house, and settled into a time of new family connections. Two years later, we bought the property from my grandparents, and they moved to another home in El Sereno. One of my fondest memories from the next six years was the Christmas Eve get-together.

My father's five living siblings (two had died in childhood and two as young adults), their spouses, and 21 first cousins would enjoy the holiday spirit. It was a magical time that would not come again, as relatives raised their own families and some moved out of the area or out of state.

Education became an important part of growing up, and I like to think that my immediate family set the stage for this. We moved to Monterey Park, and the expectation was that I would attend college-track classes in high school.

Maria Ott

One of the unusual aspects of my life is the story of how a little girl, born in Germany to the son of Mexican immigrants and a German farm girl, came to become a spokesperson for language acquisition issues and a champion of educational opportunities for all children. My story and journey began in Kronach, Germany, where I was born. My father was stationed in Germany during the Occupation, and he found his soul mate on a farm in the country outside Kronach. This is the reason I started life on German soil and learned German as my first language. When my father secured approval from the military to bring his German war bride to California to live with his family in the barrios of East Los Angeles, I became a part of the Latino culture and family that were my father's pride.

My memories of the early years in Germany are filled with connections to my mother and grandmother. I still remember the tearfilled day we left on a train to Amsterdam to board the SS Rotterdam to travel to New York. From New York to Chicago and then to Los Angeles, we traveled on a flight that took us to a strange and frightening world filled with new languages and new cultures. This first journey helped develop early resilience that would remain with me for a lifetime.

I started school as a kindergartner at Gravois Avenue School in the Los Angeles Unified School District. During the first year in Los Angeles, we lived with my father's sister and her family in a small house in the Lincoln Heights area and later with my uncle and his family in the City Terrace area. When we moved on our own, I remember the struggle of becoming part of my father's large extended family that had come to California from Chihuahua, Mexico. My father's education ended at Belvedere Junior High School, when he graduated and moved on into his life. Without a high school diploma or career training, my father moved between jobs, finally, taking trade classes to become a barber.

The large extended Gutierrez family included seven uncles and one aunt. My father was the 21st child of Maria and Jose Gutierrez, who were migrant farm workers for part of the year. Nine of their children reached adulthood, and eight were alive when I was a young child. The children born in Mexico still preferred to speak in Spanish, and all the adult males had served in the U.S. Army during World War II. Their stories of bravery were told during family picnics, and I remember my mother telling us that my uncles had survived great hardships during the war. They all viewed themselves as proud American citizens, and they wore their service to the nation as demonstration that they were part of mainstream America. Their blue-collar jobs were symbols of their success. They were proud yet humble brothers connected by their story of survival and their pride in service to a nation that had not yet found connection to a growing population of Mexican Americans.

Coming to Los Angeles immersed me into the culture of the Gutierrez family, proud Mexican Americans who maintained their roots while embracing the culture of mainstream America. My greatest challenge as a child was to learn English so that I could crawl out of the darkness of classroom instruction that assumed that every child should come to school proficient in the English language. To say that the classroom was frightening is an understatement. Sitting each day waiting to understand the teacher laid the foundation of my passion for English learners and my tenaciousness about helping all children succeed. No child should experience what welcomed me to kindergarten—the realization there was something lacking, and the lacking element was in me. Language defines you as a child, yet I was made to feel that my home language was an impediment—a problem that needed fixing.

I remember my mother trying to learn English, and this was a challenge since she had not completed her education in Germany because of the war. I remember my mother trying to learn English, and this was a challenge since she was unable to attend classes and had to learn the language on her own. The teachers at my elementary school convinced my parents that I would only succeed if all German was excluded from my life. I have always understood the meaning of sink or swim because I lived this experience. I also yearned to understand every part of my family's cultural roots. Being Mexican American during the 1950s and 1960s was a time of experiencing overt discrimination from Anglo Americans. It was also when Mexican Americans started demonstrating their cultural pride. Learning to speak Spanish helped me appreciate the richness of my father's family and past.

When I describe my language background, I acknowledge my German mother's tongue, my mastery of English, and my journey to speak Spanish to connect with my Mexican American roots. Crossing the waters from Germany to East Los Angeles was a perilous journey in many ways, yet the experiences of those early years clearly developed the tenacity and courage to lead and contribute to the improvement of public education.

Darline Robles

I will always be thankful to my mother for being my first teacher and instilling in me the desire to always do my best. My mother taught me to read early, and I was allowed to enter kindergarten earlier than most students, at the age of four.

By the time I was in fourth grade, I attended several elementary schools in Montebello, East Los Angeles (ELA), and Pico Rivera. Moving to different elementary schools taught me the importance of developing relationships, how to quickly read people and my environment, and how to adapt to new situations and to be flexible—skills that would become extremely helpful to me later on in life.

Living in a single-parent home with a working mother gave me many opportunities to demonstrate my independence. My personal drive for success came from my mother's high expectations for me and from seeing my mother working while raising her children and being independent.

I had tremendous and unconditional love and support from my mother and a very large extended family that supported all of us. One can never underestimate the value of unconditional love and support that communicates to children that we believe in them, in their dreams, and in their ability to achieve their dreams if they work hard, while knowing we are there to support them. The belief in one's self and the confidence of knowing that one is safe and loved for who she is was the grounding that I needed, and other children need, to successfully meet and navigate the challenges of growing up.

One such challenge that had a great impact on me occurred when I was in sixth grade. I was passed over for the important recognition of leading a sixth-grade May Day event. The competition involved three top students giving a speech. The three students were Sandra, a Caucasian student; Janet, a Japanese student; and me. Even though many told me that I had done the best job, I was not selected. I was stunned. It was my first school experience of rejection, and I felt it was based on my color, not on merit. The confidence that had been instilled in my ability and me did not shake my sense of self-worth. It was clear to me that not being selected to lead the May Day event was not based on ability. It was based on color. I can recall this as if it were yesterday, and this definitely influenced my teaching experiences.

In junior high school, I had close friends from different cultural backgrounds, and again, I observed different treatment of students based on cultural background, socioeconomics, and language. I realized that students who did not speak English were sent to certain classrooms in the school, and basically, they were ignored and did not mingle with other students. I realized that to make it in junior high, you had to fit in and "hang" with certain groups or be called names. In my case, even though I spoke English and did fit in, it was confusing for me to hear my peers making pejorative comments about people who looked like me and people in my family. Somehow, what was communicated to me was it was bad to be Mexican. As I look back on this experience, I know this influenced both my teaching and administrative styles to ensure that all students felt cared for, honored for who they are, and respected for what they bring to their learning.

In the ninth grade, our family moved to South El Monte, which required me to attend another school where I would have to learn to fit in. An aunt of mine was attending Sacred Heart of Mary (SHM) in Montebello, and that seemed like a better alternative to me, so with the help of my father, who convinced my mother, I applied, and was accepted into the college-prep program. I didn't know what that meant until I started school in late January. I found out that there were three educational tracks at SHM. Fortunately, I made friends quickly and got involved in choir and other school activities. Again, I observed students being treated differently based on which tracks they were enrolled in (general, business, and college-prep), which also coincided with their ethnicity and socioeconomic status. Even though the nuns were not too kind to me, I decided to stay at SHM since I had very close friends at the school. By my sophomore year, I realized I should have left. The nuns were still treating those of us who did not live in Montebello or Monterey Park as students who were less worthy of their attention. In fact, I was the only girl in the college-prep program from ELA and not from Montebello, and they did not let me forget it. One experience I remember helped me get through it. I got to know a good friend who was living at Maryvale, an orphanage for girls in Rosemead. As I got to know her and learned about her background, I realized I was fortunate to have so much in my life when others had so little. Because I was strong and confident, because I had the confidence and support of my family and friends, I knew I could make it, regardless of how others were treating me. No matter what, I knew who I was, even though others tried to ignore me or overlook my strengths and talents. I was proud to be able to take the negative treatment of me and turn it in to an opportunity to reinforce my strength.

Lessons Learned From Our Early Lives

We have reviewed and rereviewed our responses to the questions that guided the development of this book and our autobiographies, looking for themes that emerge as lessons that have informed our approaches to school leadership. From our early lives, two distinct themes emerge:

Family is important. Family has been very important to us. Even though the three of us were raised in different circumstances, in different countries and regions of the United States, we are similar in recognizing the importance of family in our formative years.

Culture is central to how we define ourselves. We recognize the importance of culture for ourselves and with our families, and we have been aware of the presence of multiple cultures in our lives.

These first two lessons learned begin a three-chapter saga of sharing our stories with you in a manner that is both descriptive and from which emerges further lessons learned. The next step in your journey with us is Chapter 3, where you will read about our early careers and the paths we have taken to this point in our lives and careers. Our interest continues to be how you and we can lead the P–12 schools to deliver high-quality education in a manner that closes achievement gaps and results in all students being able to pursue career and academic interests.

Reflection

Now that you have read about our early lives, turn your attention to your early beginnings. We are willing to bet that as you were reading about us, at times, your attention turned to your story. In the space provided, take the opportunity to reflect on the early part of your life—where you were born, something about your parents/guardians, opportunities and challenges that you encountered in your community, and recollections of your schooling. You will find these recollections informative as you construct your approach to leading in our schools today.

3

Conversations With the Superintendents

The Teacher Years

There is no teaching without learning.

Paulo Freire (1987, p. 56)

We share our stories with you expecting that, like us, you are continuously seeking ways to improve educational opportunities for all students in our schools. In this chapter, we present a discussion among ourselves facilitated by Randall Lindsey and Stephanie Graham. Randy and Stephanie are colleagues who are well schooled in topics of cultural proficiency, educational leadership, school change, and achievement gap issues.

Our process for writing this chapter occurred over six months and involved two distinct steps. First, we met several times to devise questions that would guide our personal inquiry and would inform construction of our autobiographies. These were challenging and rewarding steps because we knew we would be probing into our personal and professional lives to identify barriers we had encountered and to explore what within us allowed us to meet and transcend those challenges. Uncovering "old hurts" is not fun or easy, and there is always the question of *how much of this do we want to share with the world?* Concerns about old hurts gave way to our desire for this book to be authentic in voice and content. As you will see, we spent most of our time, as we do in our personal and professional lives, focusing on our cultural assets—the experiences and traits that enable us to overcome the identified barriers to our successes. We want you to do the same as you continue on your journey to culturally proficient leadership that promotes equitable access and outcomes for all students in our schools.

Our second step in this six-month process was to independently write responses to each of the questions we developed and to construct our autobiographies. Once the documents were in final-draft form, we passed them on to Randy and Stephanie who analyzed them for trends and themes. When they had a draft of trends among our three autobiographies and responses to the guiding questions, we conferred with Randy and Stephanie and finalized a set of themes from which we identified our "lessons learned" in Chapter 2 and which we continue to build on in this chapter and Chapter 4. The themes are described and discussed in the context of Cultural Proficiency in Chapters 5 and 6.

Following is a composite discussion among the three of us, facilitated by Randy and Stephanie, drawing on our responses to the set of questions and our autobiographies. The complete text of our responses to the guiding questions and our autobiographies is in the Resources. Topics of discussion, which appear in this chapter as subheadings, include our early lives and teachers becoming leaders. At designated points, you are provided the opportunity to reflect on our stories as well as on your professional lives and aspirations. We invite you to read our stories as if you were reading our journals. We share our stories and reflections with the hope that, like us, one's personal inquiry can be a guide to becoming an ever-effective educator and leader.

Our Early Lives

Leadership is one of those human conditions that seem to evolve throughout one's life. In constructing our personal narratives, we were interested to determine what events, if any, in our early lives might have foreshadowed or supported our futures as school leaders. Take a few moments to listen to Randy and Stephanie talk with us, Superintendents Franco, Ott, and Robles, about our early life experiences.

Randy Lindsey: *What are some of the life experiences you have had that facilitated your choice to become an educational leader?*

Carmella Franco: As both a preschooler and an elementary student, I recall being so impressed by visits to my godparents, great-aunt Susie (I received my middle name Susan from her) and great-uncle Ben's home in Pueblo, Colorado. There I would sit and listen to Uncle Ben play ragtime-style piano on an old upright. The piano was located in their basement, which also housed a boxing gym where kids from the neighborhood hung out. I watched Uncle Ben give them boxing tips, and would also flip through the boxing magazines stacked in a corner of the gym. Little did I know, these two experiences, grounded in my hometown of Pueblo, would have a profound effect in facilitating my rise to becoming an educational leader.

My parents, Al and Margaret, although very young in their parenting role, decided to nurture my interests by buying me an upright piano for my seventh birthday. By this time, we had moved to join my paternal grandparents who had moved from Las Palomas, New Mexico, to Los Angeles, California. I began my study of piano with teacher Velta Barviks at the Los Angeles Music and Art School (LAMAS), a wonderful community arts facility founded by Pearle Irene Odell.

These lessons would later come into play as I progressed in my career and pursued a doctorate. From music, I learned

Self-discipline and the setting of goals

Persistence and determination

Development of a lifelong hobby

Lessons from boxing came into play. I learned to

Plan strategies carefully

Size up my opponent (person or concept)

Adjust as the fight unfolds

Never give up on what I'm fighting for

Get back up and regroup whenever I'm knocked down

Learn from the losses

Maria Ott: On a personal level, I believe that my journey to learn English and succeed as a student both at the elementary and secondary levels built deep compassion for students who are taking the same journey to succeed academically. It is interesting when I hear others describe their kindergarten and first-grade experiences, and all I have is darkness. The darkness reflects the fear and anxiety that accompanied my introduction to school, a new culture, and a new, extended family.

When my mother, brother, and I arrived from Germany, I was five years old, and we moved in with my father's sister and her family in East Los Angeles. The house was too small to accommodate all of us comfortably, but my father's family made the best of the difficult arrangement. Eventually, my father was able to rent a small house near his sister. I started kindergarten at Gravois Avenue Elementary School, moving on to Sacred Heart Catholic School. The only memories that remain from those early days in school are recollections of uncomfortable situations. I still remember coming home with a worksheet that had my last name misspelled, and I repeated to my mother how my teacher said my name was pronounced. My mother was upset that the teacher did not get my name right. When she told me that the teacher was wrong, I cried. "How could my teacher be wrong?" I thought.

In elementary school, I acquired tenacity about doing well in school, and I would stay up late, trying to get my schoolwork right. I remember my parents talking to my teachers about my habit of erasing my work until it was right. That is why many of my papers ended up with holes from erasures. My mother had the job of trying to help with my homework, which was frustrating for both of us since my mother's education from Germany was different in content and method from what was expected in my classes. It was only after having my children that I learned how important the homework experience is for children. My parents were incredibly supportive in that they insisted that I do my best in school, wanting more for me than was available in their school years. The fact that homework is a cultural experience for mainstream American students should not be overlooked when thinking about ways to help English learners and children who are socioeconomically disadvantaged.

Darline Robles: Upon entering college, I had an interest in three careers, a lawyer, a psychologist, and a teacher. Right after high school, I was hired as a playground assistant director for Pico Rivera Parks and Recreation. I was assigned to Pio Pico Elementary School. This neighborhood was known for its poverty and very gang-involved families. Children who attended Pio Pico were known as troublemakers, and when I was hired, I was told that I probably could not get them involved in the many activities offered to the children through Parks and Recreation. When I began working in the summer, I was very excited about developing a great summer program. The director at the site allowed me to create the program to fit the needs of the community (e.g., sport, crafts, field trips, anything that would bring the kids to the playground from 10 a.m. to 6 p.m. every day). The children came every day and participated in all the activities, and that was when realized I really wanted to teach. During the next several years at Pio Pico Parks and Recreation, the program was known as one of the best in the city. It was a program where the children felt they belonged, they felt cared for, and they felt success every day they participated in the program. I learned that with the right motivation and program elements, all children will participate and learn. I knew that I had had a hand in developing the success of the program and in making a difference in the lives of the children who participated in the program. It was one of the best jobs I ever had.

Having learned so much from my mother, being a good student myself, and wanting success for students like me and the ones I was working with at Pio Pico shaped my decision to become a teacher.

Stephanie Graham: *Describe ways you have achieved equitable recognition, visibility, opportunities, identity formation, and balance in your personal and professional life.*

Franco: It was important that, first, women be accorded the same opportunities as men. Second, it was critical that *women of color* be viewed as competent leaders, selected on the basis to lead an organization. In four of the organizations to which I achieved this end, the majority of the membership was white.

Even with such a goal, I have never worn a label of identity formation. I view myself first as having been a successful superintendent and educational leader. This included being a role model for employees, for community members, and, most important, for the students. It is to be noted that an all-white board hired me because I met everything they were looking for in a superintendent. That I happened to be Hispanic proved to be the icing on the cake.

It is difficult to strike a balance between the professional and the personal. Many sacrifices have been made during my career, in particular ones involving family. One can certainly attempt to lessen the impact; however, there will be sacrifices. A vivid example of this goes back to the first four months of my superintendency in Whittier City School District. On the night my contract was approved, the board also approved moving forward with a bond. I found myself being in the community 43 of 46 nights. Is that balance? No—I did what was needed, and luckily, the bond passed. It would have been deadly for me to have my first major challenge as a superintendent fail. I went in running and stayed running—that epitomizes my 12 years in that position.

Ott: My English teacher Sister Redempta introduced me to English literature, poetry, and expository and creative writing. This is when I learned that English was more than diagramming sentences and writing reports. Sister Redempta taught me to love the English language and to use it as a tool for life.

By high school, I learned the rules and was navigating toward college. I met my future husband while attending high school, and he was a source of encouragement when I decided to apply to Mount St. Mary's College, in Los Angeles.

Mount St. Mary's College has a long tradition of opening the doors of opportunity for minority women, especially Latinas. The school's success has earned the college a record of excellence for women breaking through the barriers of poverty and opening career opportunities. I consider the decision to attend Mount St. Mary's College life altering. My life was like a paper canoe sailing down the river of experience, and Mount St. Mary's turned that paper canoe into a well-armed warship ready to take on the challenges of a career, marriage, motherhood, and public service. The English courses continued my enthusiasm for literature and creative writing started at San Gabriel Mission High School.

Robles: In 1967, I met my future husband, and in 1969, we were married. By 1969, I left my job at the playground and focused on completing my studies. During this time, my husband Frank supported my decision to continue attending school, even though it would be harder once my son was born in 1970. In 1972, I finally achieved my goal, and received a BA in history, and now, I was determined to get my elementary credential. Finances prevented me from thinking about a master's degree, but in time, I heard about the support provided for students entering the Teacher Corps program at the University of Southern California (USC). Since my husband was the only one working, and because I did not want to apply for loans, I would need some kind of assistance to continue my studies. In June 1972, I was accepted into the Teacher Corps program at USC. At the end of the two years, I would earn a master's degree in urban education and a teaching credential.

During the summer and fall, I worked in Pasadena doing field-work and taught at Los Padrinos Juvenile Hall and Bunche Junior High in Compton. Many of the Chicanos in the program, including myself, were interested in working in bilingual settings or English as a second language (ESL) classes as part of our experience. However, we were told by the program administrators that they did not see the importance of such a focus. We were shocked by the response.

We tried to get local, state, and national support for our concerns but to no avail. Our demonstrations in front of the dean's office did not make an impact. Nine of us decided to leave the program, with some of us eventually completing our studies at Claremont Graduate School, which offered the best options for us. We fought for recognition of our culture and identity, and we took a stand. This same issue has come up several times in my career, of course, with different details. But the questions are always the same: Who are we? Are we recognized for who we are, and what do we stand for? Do we settle for less? These questions and the pursuit of just answers to them were and are driving forces in my life. The dogged pursuit of educational equity and social justice has a price. Trying to do the right thing for the right kids can take time and effort away from tending to one's family, and it can jeopardize professional aspirations if organizational leaders do not agree with one's equity agenda. Balancing the demands of one's personal convictions with one's professional goals is a challenge. But at the end of the day, who are we as family members, and as professionals, if we are not better individuals ourselves for making the world a better place for those whose voices are not heard and needs are not recognized in schools and in society?

Reflection

What do you see as trends or themes in these superintendents' early lives that might have supported their emergence as school leaders? Thinking about your early life, what are some occurrences that have influenced you to become an educator and a leader?

_____

_____

_____

_____

Teachers Becoming Leaders

Teachers are natural leaders in their classroom, and they function as formal and nonformal leaders when networking with teacher colleagues, teacher aides, counselors, administrators, parents, and members of the community. Recognizing one's desire to be a formal leader and/or being recognized by one's peers for leadership traits are often precursors to a teacher pursuing an advanced degree and required certification to become a school administrator.

Graham: *Describe the day you decided you wanted to become a school leader.*

Ott: I remember attending a church social event in high school. My father was to pick me up, and as he waited in the church parking lot, a group of young, white males insulted him by calling him a "beaner." My father was fuming when I came to the car. The restraint that he used in not starting a problem was a tribute to his desire to do what was best for his children. My blood boils every time that I think of that night. How dare anyone insult my hardworking father. Beaner was a term used to insult and let a Mexican American know how he or she was viewed.

When I ask myself why I have such a sense of urgency about my work, I know that each experience left a mark. Most of life's day-to-day activities are easily forgotten, yet hurtful and embarrassing situations sting even in our senior years. We have the wisdom to understand ignorance, intolerance, and fear; however, the desire to prevent these hurtful experiences from touching other lives seems only to grow stronger with age. I often ask myself if I will ever be able to let it go.

After my marriage, my husband started teaching at a Catholic K–8 school while attending Loyola University to work on his master's degree in English. One of his students struggled with English. She was an eighth-grade immigrant in need of tutoring and English language instruction. My husband asked if I would help this student, and the experience was the cure for my dilemma regarding becoming a leader. I felt needed and rewarded by working with this young lady, and I became increasingly interested in my husband's experiences in the classroom.

I was disturbed that many of my students were labeled special education when their real need was for effective instruction to help them reach grade-level expectations in English. In 1975, PL 94-142 became effective, opening the door to better understanding of special education students' needs and appropriate intervention. There have been positives and negatives since passage of federal law to ensure that eligible students are appropriately educated. I witnessed first-hand students who were labeled inappropriately, and I taught my class as if my students were gifted and talented, and they behaved like the best students in the entire school.

During April of 1971, I asked the principal if I could work with my students in Spanish as preparation for Cinco de Mayo, a symbolic celebration of pride for Mexican Americans. The principal wanted to be supportive so he gave me permission to use Spanish but cautioned that I could only use Spanish for this assignment and activities. The students were so proud of their work in their native language. I could see great potential hidden under the label of low expectations by a system that did not know how to respond to a growing immigrant population.

In spring 1972, I read an announcement in the Los Angeles Unified School District (LAUSD) newsletter that there were openings in a bilingual program funded by federal Title VII resources. Teachers bilingual in Spanish could apply and would have to pass a proficiency test to demonstrate bilingual competence. I decided to apply and took the test, receiving the highest ranking of A-level fluency in Spanish. I interviewed at three schools and received three employment offers. One of the schools was in my old neighborhood on the East side of Los Angeles. City Terrace Elementary School was my choice, and I was assigned to a second-grade classroom.

Robles: I recall one day when my principal stated he did not want me to leave the classroom and take on a special assignment position at the district office. I was so upset that one individual could make that decision for me that could affect my professional growth. That was when I realized that could never happen again. I was committed to making sure that I was in control of my professional growth, and to do that, I must be in the role of a leader.

Franco: The day I decided to become a school leader stands out vividly in my mind. I determined that I wanted to become a teacher when I was in seventh grade. This was because I really enjoyed school and my teachers called on me often to tutor fellow classmates who were struggling with their reading or math.

I had such positive experiences with my elementary school teachers that it was inevitable that I would decide to become a teacher. The years of serving as a "teacher's helper" and classroom tutor for those who needed extra assistance paved the way for me.

My decision to become a school leader, however, took place in other circumstances. As a music major in college, I was studying with Dr. Milton Stern at California State University, Los Angeles (CSULA). It was my second year—I was 19 years old. Sometime during the lesson, Dr. Stern asked me about my career goals. I answered that I wanted to become a school principal. This decision preceded becoming a public school teacher. In essence, I already knew that I wanted to lead. From the solitary experience with my piano, I wanted to expand to lead others. In a reflective sense, the inner strength developed, waiting to be of use.

Lindsey: *In what ways did your gender enhance or limit access to your early leadership roles?*

Robles: Early in my career, I found support and recognition from my peers and supervisors. The administrative team at Montebello Office of Instruction (MOI) (the school district is Montebello Unified School District, Montebello, California) was in my classroom on a regular basis and provided me with the feedback for growth. I took advantage of every professional development opportunity. I took leadership assignments, worked in the afternoon with English learners, and was able to provide professional development on ESL strategies to teachers. I became very involved with the parent council, and supported efforts to provide training to our parents.

After a few years, I was able to help implement the district's first bilingual/bicultural program for sixth to eighth grade. Around this time, I accepted a special assignment at the central office working with the coordinator of bilingual education. As a young Latina working with mostly white administrators, now at the district level, I knew how important but also how risky it was for me to navigate the cultural and political differences in the district.

When I returned to the classroom, I was asked to take on the assignment of Child Welfare and Attendance Supervisor (CWA). I learned another part of the school that I had only observed from the perspective of a classroom teacher. Here, I worked with counselors, teachers, parents, and the entire administrative team to improve the attendance of students.

Franco: The teachers invariably called on girls to serve in classroom leadership roles. I was always selected to lead projects, from overseeing the construction of a castle and moat (studying the Middle Ages) to correcting papers of spelling and math tests. As part of the project phase, I had to select other students who I thought could successfully work as a team. This was a challenge, as everyone wanted to be called on to participate. In retrospect, this leadership role provided training for personnel selection later on in my career. My classmates called me "the professor," a nickname that helped nudge me along the route to becoming a teacher. My gender definitely enhanced my access to leadership roles. I do not recall any boys ever being given this opportunity during my elementary school years.

I encountered major barriers because of gender. In my second year of teaching, I made an appointment with human resources (personnel, in those days), and when I stated that I had the goal of becoming a principal, I was told, "Why would a nice, young woman like you want to be a principal?" Still, I requested that I be considered at some future time. That same month, I went to CSULA to investigate entering the administrative credential master's degree program. An appointment had been set with the dean of the department, which was all male. Again, I was told that I was only 23 years old. I was told to obtain an MA in another curricular area and then come back. I knew I had the gift of time, so I did just that. I obtained an MA in elementary education, focused some of my research on women in administration, and then returned to pursue my administrative credential. The number of women in the classes had increased to about 20%. The second time around, I encountered no objections from the dean.

Ott: Gender surfaced during my first assignment as principal. I was the first woman assigned to Hart Street School in Canoga Park, most of the administrators in the area were male, and they were fond of reminding me and the other new female administrators that we were not part of the club. The comments did not bother me because I felt that my appointment as principal was evidence that I was on an equal footing with my male counterparts. Sometimes comments were made that would be considered sexist now; however, at that time, males behaved in ways that were offensive but accepted in the workplace. I remember being introduced as someone who was "good looking." Good looking had nothing to do with my success in the exam process for principal, so I just disregarded the remarks.

Later, when I was selected as the superintendent for the Little Lake City School District, the headline in the local newspaper read

"Latina Appointed." I was the first woman to lead the district, and I was also the first person of color. On a personal level, being the "first woman" was reflection of my hard work and talent, and I did not feel the impediments that many women of my era described.

The reason that being a woman limited access was more at the personal level because I was trying to have it all—a successful career and a successful personal life. This was the hardest part of being a woman in a leadership role.

When I read the research about women who attend single-gender schools, I learned that my years at a coinstitutional high school where all the girls attended separate classrooms from the boys prepared me to be successful. The fact that I attended a college for women also prepared me to succeed in a profession dominated by male leadership. I was educated to believe in myself and to tackle any challenge to make a difference that would matter to society. Attending Mount Saint Mary's College was truly an experience that would alter my career potential. Not only was I the first in my family to attend college but also I benefited from an education designed to help women succeed in life and in their careers.

Graham: *How did your culture enhance or limit access to your early leadership roles?*

Franco: I was an English-only speaker, one of a few in my school setting. My proficiency in English, both spoken and written, probably placed me at an advantage in a school that was at least 95% Hispanic. I did not feel at a disadvantage not knowing Spanish, as none of the teachers knew it either. However, my ear was tuned to it; I wanted to learn the language; and I ultimately learned it, beginning in fifth grade. I carried a Spanish/English dictionary with me everywhere I went. My paternal grandmother, Teresa Torres Padilla, played an important role in assisting me with this goal. It took some convincing on my part, as she spoke only English to her more than 20 grandchildren. From college until her passing, we spoke nearly daily—in Spanish!

From first grade on, each of my elementary school teachers encouraged me to succeed. By all accounts, I was an overachiever, eager to please, and I was told that I would go far in life.

Ott: The greatest obstacle that I faced in relationship to my culture was overcoming expectations. As the oldest child in the Gutierrez family, I had no role models that were available to guide me as I prepared to graduate from a Catholic high school. My teachers helped me shape dreams of a better life. My parents were hardworking, saving to pay for Catholic schooling at the elementary and secondary level. As an adult, I have come to appreciate the sacrifices made by my parents. My father worked as a barber, and he worked six days a week to make a living. My mother was frugal, and saved by making all the clothes for the family and preparing economical meals. The humble beginnings of both my parents, and our humble lifestyle, produced four successful adults; three of the four graduated from college. I earned a PhD, and I continue to attribute my success to the hard work that characterized every aspect of my upbringing.

My father's family came to the United States during the Mexican Revolution in search of work and a better life for their children. The Gutierrez family was large, and they valued their time together. Typically, the family gathered for picnics in the park to celebrate special events—birthdays, holidays, and bridal and baby showers. I remember feeling most accepted for who I was when I was with my cousins. There were no pretenses, and we were proud to be Mexican Americans.

Since culture defines us, I believe that my early leadership roles were positively influenced by the work ethic, appreciation for being Mexican American, and the respect for my first culture (German) that were demonstrated in my family. We struggled economically, yet we were rich in life experiences.

Robles: At the time I accepted a special assignment at the central office working with the coordinator of bilingual education, it was clear that my proud cultural heritage, my knowledge of the students' home cultures, was an asset. The backdrop of state and federal support for "limited English proficient speakers" helped me address the concerns and soften the resistance of the naysayers in the district. As a young Latina working with mostly white administrators, now at the district level, I knew how important but also how risky it was for me to navigate the cultural and political differences in the district. I knew I had to garner support from allies and address the concerns of detractors whether they were staff members, elected officials, or policy makers to ensure quality programs for English learners. This was risky business for a young Latina professional such as me. But something deep inside me bolstered my confidence. The values and beliefs passed to me by strong and proud family members who cared for me deeply and expected great things from me, strengthened my resolve to make a life-changing difference in the lives of bicultural/bilingual students.

Lindsey: *Describe the role of mentors at this stage of your career.*

Ott: In fall of 1978, my former principal at Sierra Vista Elementary School was assigned as principal to Murchison Elementary School, serving the area that included the Ramona Gardens Housing Project. He asked that I be assigned as his vice principal. The need for a strong leadership team for Murchison was a priority for Region G Superintendent Bill Anton, and he made a special personnel assignment that allowed my appointment without the regular promotional exam process.

I served as vice principal for more than three years, moving the school from traditional to year-round calendar, and improving achievement and student safety. In 1981, I took the principals exam and placed in the top 5%. The experiences of working in an area of high-crime statistics and at a low-achieving school serving many recent immigrants and students with high levels of poverty convinced me that leadership was essential to building a strong culture of teaching and learning. My principal was an outstanding instructional leader, and I learned about leadership under his mentorship. He taught me that the role of the principal was to keep focus, coherency, and priorities. I learned that it is not possible to do everything well, so I had to select the areas that make the greatest impact on the quality of teaching and learning to ensure that my efforts made a difference for students. Working under this mentor helped me become a strong principal.

Later in my career, I was blessed to find outstanding Latinas who served as my mentors and guided me to realize that I could become a superintendent. My first significant mentor was Amelia McKenna who was an associate superintendent in LAUSD. Amelia McKenna demonstrated her expertise in multiple leadership roles, and she was acknowledged across the school district as a leader to be respected and admired. She selected me as an administrator in her division, which was responsible for all language acquisition issues in the LAUSD. I remember working with Amelia McKenna as one of the most rewarding experiences of my career. Ms. McKenna had a brave heart for children learning English as a second language and for children of poverty. Like me, Amelia McKenna was a Latina with interesting cultural roots, descending from a Scotsman who worked building the railroad in Mexico. Amelia McKenna trusted my judgment, and we became an inseparable team for the children in LAUSD who needed advocates at the top of the LAUSD organization.

Robles: After I served a year as the CWA supervisor, I returned to the classroom. That year, we had a new district bilingual coordinator, Dr. Mary Gonzales Mend. Dr. Mend had been the first Latina principal in Montebello USD. When Dr. Mend asked me to take on the assignment of professional development services member, a teacher on special assignment, I was excited about the opportunity, much to the protestation of my principal! Dr. Mend was eventually able to get me released, and I served two years with Dr. Mend, where I learned so much. I had never worked for a woman supervisor before, and felt so fortunate to learn from her and from other women on the team who remain good friends and colleagues to this day. It was during this tenure that I gained full awareness of my culture and my gender as strengths of leadership. I knew the challenges to the successful leadership journeys of so many women like me, and realized that I had a responsibility as a trailblazer and as sister to mentor them, so that they, too, could embrace their gender and culture, related wisdom, knowledge, and disposition.

Franco: As a teacher, I was thrown into leadership roles beginning my second year. That year, the teacher union asked me to be on the team that wrote the first teacher contract for Rowland Unified School District. I spent countless nights at the local California Teachers' Association (CTA) offices being trained on how to construct the contract. In another occurrence, my peers at the site elected me one of their representatives to the School Advisory Committee (SAC). This experience enhanced my interactions with parents, colleagues, and district office staff. Additionally, my principal placed me in charge of multicultural activities (Cinco de Mayo) and other performances for parents.

My visibility and expertise caught the eye of the new assistant superintendent of instruction, and I was ultimately selected for a position in the reorganized division. It was an ideal time, with instruction the number one focus. The development of the new cadre of specialists became a work in progress. I benefited greatly by gaining experience in a multitude of areas: intermediate level science adoption; high school course revision process; nurses' handbook (revision); assisting with staff development activities for teachers, principals, and other administrators.

Lessons Learned From Our Careers

Themes have emerged as lessons during the early part of our careers to inform our approaches to education from our beginning as teachers and, ultimately, as teacher leaders. Two themes from our early lives have been reinforced, and a new theme has emerged:

Family is important. Our extended families were a source of support and encouragement during our early days as educators, and they provided balance throughout our careers.

Culture is central to how we define ourselves. We recognize the importance of how ethnicity and gender as culture are viewed and experienced by those who have hindered or facilitated our careers.

Multiple mentors are indispensable. Mentoring is crucial to overcoming barriers, and it emanates from different directions and sources. Similarly, cross-cultural mentoring, from men and women of other racial and ethnic groups, helped introduce us to the organizational cultures of successful leadership.

Reflection

This section was packed with information, and it may take several minutes to digest. What trends or themes do you see from the early parts of our careers that might have supported our progression as school leaders? Thinking about the early phases of your career, what are some occurrences that have supported your role as school leader?

4

Conversations With the Superintendents

The Administrator Years

Those who say it can't be done should get out of the way of those who are doing it.

Joel Barker (1996)

We continue sharing our stories with you through focusing on our years as school administrators. In this chapter, we continue the discussion among ourselves facilitated by Randall Lindsey and Stephanie Graham. As with Chapter 3, our process for writing this chapter occurred over six months and involved two distinct steps.

- Initially, we met to devise questions to guide our personal inquiry and to inform the development of our autobiographies. You may recall from Chapter 3 that these were challenging and rewarding steps because of probing into our personal and professional lives to uncover barriers we had encountered and to discover what within us allowed us to meet and rise above those challenges. When reading the passages in this chapter, you will notice that we confronted some "old hurts," for this book to be authentic in voice and content. Once the old hurts have been identified, we focus on our cultural assets—the experiences and traits that enable us to overcome the identified barriers to our successes. We invite you to do the same as you continue on your journey to culturally proficient leadership that promotes equitable access and outcomes for all students in our schools.

- As described in the opening to Chapter 3, our second step in this process was to independently write responses to each of the questions and to construct our autobiographies. Once the documents were in final-draft form, Randy and Stephanie analyzed the documents for trends and themes, and from the analysis emerged "lessons learned" in Chapters 2 and 3, which we continue to build on in this chapter. The themes are further developed, described, and discussed within the context of the Tools of Cultural Proficiency in Chapters 5 and 6.

Randy and Stephanie continue the composite discussion from Chapter 3, drawing on our responses to the set of questions and our autobiographies. The complete text of our responses to the guiding questions and our autobiographies is in the Resources. Topics of discussion, which appear in this chapter as subheadings, include our early administrative roles and our superintendent roles. At designated points, you are provided the opportunity to reflect on our stories as well as on your professional life and aspirations. We invite you to read our stories as if you were reading our journals. If our stories are a guide to your becoming an ever-effective educator and leader, we will be greatly fulfilled.

Administrative Roles

Earning the requisite college degrees and state/provincial certification to serve as a school administrator are the visible components to acquiring and being successful in one's entry-level positions. However, possessing the qualities of a leader, being recognized for having those qualities, and being mentored (formally or informally) are instrumental to early successes as a school administrator.

Graham: *What do you see as your strong personal qualities that helped you in your initial leadership position?*

Robles: My strongest personal qualities are interpersonal skills. Again, I believe you must connect with the people around you—even if they don't want to connect with you. As a teacher leader, bilingual coordinator, and elementary principal, I had to work with many individuals who did not want to change their instructional strategies to meet the changing student demographics. To move the staff in each of these settings, I had to build a relationship and provide a supportive environment, where they would be willing to try new behaviors and meet the student needs. Another personal quality is demanding the best from me and from others on behalf of all students and having high standards for everyone in the profession. And I have integrity. And I usually stay very calm under stressful situations. A newscaster once asked me if I was a Marine. He had just seen me be grilled by elected officials, and I responded to each question in a calm and respectful manner. He told me that he was in awe by my calmness, and thought I had to be a Marine to have remained so calm. I am also persistent in achieving my goals.

Franco: I entered an administrative credential program at age 25, and completed it two years later. I obtained my first administrative position as a bilingual/English as Second Language (ESL) specialist at age 27. Some of the personal qualities that helped me with that entry position included the following:

- Knowledge about the area of specialty (e.g., I taught in the district's first Title VII bilingual program for four years)
- A sense of political awareness (e.g., I made a point of introducing myself to principals and senior managers so they knew who I was and had also met several board members)
- Persistence in the pursuit of my career goals (e.g., I mapped paths for achieving my career goals)
- Support from a mentor

Assistant Superintendent Dr. Dolores Smith became a mentor at work. She signed me up for my first Association of California School Administrators (ACSA) Committee, and made sure that I joined the Women in Educational Leadership (WEL) organization based in Los Angeles. That also started my lifelong involvement in organizations, which would prove extremely important and fulfilling as I moved through leadership roles.

Ott: Because I experienced prejudice and intolerance as a young adult, I acquired a deep and unwavering sense of compassion and commitment to children who were learning English and who were striving to be the first in their families to graduate from high school and go on to college. I always share my personal story of struggle and success with families in my community so that I will be a role model that inspires others to succeed. For many young women who have not known role models from their culture, it is crucial for them to know what I have overcome to be a successful educator. I feel a sense of obligation that by sharing my story, I am influencing young women to strive for higher levels in their career aspirations.

I had only been the principal at Sheridan for two years when I was offered the opportunity to take a promotional assignment as a director of instruction for another area of the school district. After giving the offer a thorough review, I declined the promotion. My belief was that someone leading instruction for other principals should have demonstrated that she could move a school to new levels of achievement. Colleagues and supervisors told me that I had made an error in turning down this opportunity—one does not turn down a promotion. I still find it interesting that I was not commended for wanting to become a stronger leader before promoting. Although I had been a principal for four years, I had not been at one school long enough to demonstrate the outcomes of my instructional leadership to a level that I considered acceptable to lead other administrators.

I have never regretted the decision to pass on my first promotional opportunity since the additional three years as principal at Sheridan led the school to new heights of effectiveness. When the second promotion was offered, I accepted the role as administrator for the Eastman Curriculum Design Project, which had started as a research-based design at Eastman Elementary School and was expanded to 28 schools.

I was appointed the lead administrator, and was responsible for a staff of four teacher advisers, two secretaries, and the work of one researcher.

Lindsey: *Did you have formal or informal mentors? If yes, how did they support you? In what ways did your gender or culture enhance or limit your access to mentoring?*

Franco: I observed from the start that I would need to prove myself doubly in every administrative position. I made sure that I had all the credentials; I attended workshop after workshop designed for women who wanted to succeed and, in effect, break through the glass ceiling; I observed those female leaders who had made it to the ranks of senior management. None were Hispanic, so I had no role models in that regard other than some in the Los Angeles Unified School District (LAUSD) system who were involved with WEL.

One of my mentors, via the University of La Verne (ULV) doctoral program, was Dr. Patricia Clark White, who was a superintendent in Orange County, California. She served as a member of my dissertation committee, and was the first person I called when I obtained my superintendent position.

Beyond that, I have been mentoring many participants from diverse backgrounds in the ACSA Superintendents Academy who aspire to senior management and superintendent positions. I currently serve as one of the directors for this particular academy, and this gives me an opportunity to encourage and assist those who are interested in expanded leadership responsibilities.

Ott: I always had informal mentors. When it became apparent that mentoring was important for women and persons of color, I had already reached the level of principal, so I became a formal mentor for others.

The Ford Foundation funded a University of Southern California (USC) led program with the goal of increasing Latino teachers by supporting Latino instructional aides in pursuing their college diplomas and teaching credentials. The findings from this work demonstrated that mentoring was a powerful component in the success of the participants. The support of family and colleagues was integral to goal attainment for the participants. Serving in an advisory role to this project, I realized that I had overcome significant traditional barriers without formal support from a mentoring system.

During this time, I helped launch the mentoring program for aspiring administrators started by the LAUSD Council of Mexican American Administrators. As a formal mentor, I was able to help women and other Latinos strive for advancement in the LAUSD promotional system. It was most gratifying helping others increase their personal qualities of leadership.

When I was president of the California Association of Latino Superintendents and Administrators (CALSA), I met Dr. Ken Magdaleno who was a graduate student working on research related to mentoring to increase the ranks of Latino administrators. His doctoral work became the foundation for one of the most successful mentoring programs for Latinos and women. I am currently mentoring a talented African American woman who is a successful principal and who aspires to become a superintendent.

Robles: I have been fortunate to have many mentors—both informal and formal. Part of my personality is to seek out individuals who have the skills and talents I need to build in myself. When I find that individual, I ask for their help. I am not afraid of asking for help. In one way, I think my gender has been an asset in accessing mentoring. I just think men are more hesitant to ask for help than women. As for my culture, I don't think it has limited my access to mentoring.

Reflection

Once again, this section has much information. What trends or themes from the middle phases of our careers might have supported our movement into formal leadership roles as school administrators? If you are an experienced educator, what are some experiences that have supported your role as school leader, whether from the role of teacher, counselor, or administrator? If you are in the first phase of your career as an educator, what are you taking from this section to incorporate into your *professional plan*?

_____

_____

_____

_____

The Superintendency

From the classroom to the superintendency often entails serving in many administrative roles. Given the complexity of modern education, school administrators must be informed about all aspects of schooling—curriculum, instruction, professional development, assessment and accountability, parent/community outreach and communication, human and resource allocations, public relations, safety, and internal and external politics are examples of the many layers of the job. Mastering each of these roles involves a learning curve, and it is done with societal pressures. Being a woman and/or person of color in school administration has often created a complex context for administrators such as Superintendents Franco, Ott, and Robles.

Graham: *What do you see as your strong personal qualities that helped you break through barriers to becoming a superintendent?*

Ott: In 1993, I received a call from my mentor encouraging me to apply for the superintendent vacancy in the Little Lake City School District. The district was small, serving 5,400 students in the cities of Santa Fe Springs, northern Norwalk, and southeastern Downey. My first reaction to this encouragement was that I could not see myself as a superintendent, and I certainly did not see myself leaving my career in LAUSD. In retrospect, I realize that my reluctance to being open to this opportunity was born from my fear of not being worthy. When children grow up in disadvantaged circumstances, they carry self-doubts. Although I had a successful career, I questioned whether I could be an effective superintendent. This self-doubt was a remnant of my early struggles to learn English and do well in school.

The work in LAUSD was perhaps the most challenging of my career. As a nontraditional superintendent, the LAUSD board required that Roy Romer find an educational deputy to help him run the district. I accepted the deputy position with the commitment that I would do everything possible to help Romer succeed as superintendent. I remembered how difficult it had been for Leonard Britton to succeed when he assumed the LAUSD superintendent's position in July 1987. Coming from outside the system presented unique challenges for any new superintendent. My gift to Romer was my unwavering loyalty.

During the five years I spent as Romer's senior deputy superintendent, I learned about the power of clear communication and the power of weaving stories into your message to create images that help people understand your intent. Romer was a skilled communicator, and he was a strong leader who drove his agenda through a centralized approach. It was my role to help the organization move forward with Romer's priorities. Fortunately, Romer made instruction his priority. Early in his superintendency, we discussed the legacy he hoped to leave. His aspiration was to leave a legacy of improved instruction. I explained that to accomplish lasting instructional change in LAUSD, he would have to commit to more than three years. I stayed with Romer for five years, and he remained an additional year, serving more than six years as superintendent.

Starting as superintendent in Rowland Unified in 2005, the first order of business was to listen and learn the culture of my new district while building relationships with staff and the community. The superintendent's cabinet included four assistant superintendents with extensive careers in the district. The least veteran member of the cabinet had more than 10 years in the district. The other three had been in the district more than 30 years. This experienced team could have made my transition difficult; however, I found a group of dedicated individuals who would help me during my first 90 days and beyond. They advised me on the traditions of the Rowland Unified School District and helped me analyze the needs of the district.

Robles: An additional personal quality that was not mentioned previously is my willingness to take risks. If I had been timid or averse to risks, I would never have been willing to become the interim superintendent in Montebello USD. When I was asked to take this position, the district was close to being taken over by the state, and we had to cut more than 30% of the budget to survive. My willingness to take this on, as my first superintendency, demonstrates my courage and risk-taking qualities.

Franco: I believe my strong personal qualities include the following:

- *Persistence.* As noted earlier, when dissuaded from entering the administrative credential program, I made a brief detour, and then successfully returned to my goal. I put on blinders when I began work on my doctorate. I completed the required three years of coursework, and wound up in the top 5% of the class. It's recommended that doctoral candidates take 18 to 24 months to complete the dissertation. I wrote mine in eight months, something I do not recommend to others. It was good to have it completed, however.

  My husband, family, and friends were especially supportive of my goals. During the doctoral work, I became acutely aware of something: I could count the number of Hispanics on one hand, and that was out of nearly 200 in the cohort. It was a self-mandate to excel and represent my ethnic and cultural group well. Beyond that, I was self-motivated and self-driven, and the drive to succeed was heavily intrinsic.
- *Competence.* It was important that all credentials were obtained, including the doctorate. There should be no question regarding my competence in the field. The administrative paths that I pursued enhanced my preparation as a principal, a director, and, ultimately, a superintendent.

- *Demand the best.* I demanded the best from and had high expectations of both others and myself. For example, the image of the school district was a major responsibility. I was known for editing, and the dreaded "red pen." This included, in particular, presentations to the board. I often perused budget presentations, finding items that needed editing or correction. As time passed, in my superintendency, I finally gave myself some latitude to err.
- *Hard worker.* This is best exemplified by the General Obligation Bond and Mello-Roos Bond, which entailed me being out in the community nearly every night and on weekends. My visibility in Whittier helped contribute to a more positive view of the school district, which facilitated the passage of two bond issues.
- *Visionary.* One thing near and dear to my heart was the importance of libraries in the schools. In partnership with the Rose Hills Foundation and the hard work of the principals, between 2001 and 2008, when I retired, each of the elementary schools enjoyed a brand new library.

I wanted the school district to provide every opportunity for students to have above and beyond the "normal" school experience. Overseeing the securing of 12 million dollars in outside funds (e.g., grants) helped to accomplish this end.

- *Excellent communicator.* The development of strategies to relay the school district's message was critical. This included oral and written communications (e.g., polished newsletters) along with personal interactions.
- *Collaborator and bridge builder.* Working closely with government agencies, both state and city, and employee groups over the years contributed to a successful tenure as superintendent. This was carried out further when I was selected interim superintendent of the Woodland Joint Unified School District. While there was not always agreement, there was certainly a respect for differing opinions and a genuine effort on my part for all to work together in a collaborative fashion in the best interest of students.
- *Ability to work well with boards of education.* With a few exceptions, and only where board member egos interfered, the relationship between the superintendent and the board was one where I worked tirelessly. There was frequent turnover at election time in Whittier, and it was incumbent on me to know the

board members and build relationships. I am grateful to the board that hired me and, after that, to several who were particularly supportive of my efforts to serve the students and their families. During my interim superintendency in Woodland, I enjoyed building relationships with the seven-member board. It proved to be an eventful, challenging, and magical year, and I am thankful for the opportunity the board provided to me.

If I had to cite a facet of my style that contributed to good board/superintendent relations, it would be equitable and fair treatment of the individual members, whether I agreed with them or not. Additionally, relationships were kept professional, no matter who came on and off the board.

- *See both sides of issues.* The ability to stand back, cross over the fence, and stand in the other person or organization's shoes is one of my greatest strengths. It contributed to a sense of empathy and understanding. I spent much time on this with my senior managers, helping them to see the benefits of doing so.

- *Make hard decisions.* I have always said that I was not in my position to win a popularity contest. Feathers were ruffled and feelings were hurt, no doubt, in the quest to achieve excellence and meet students' educational needs. We all want to be liked; however, many superintendents sacrifice their integrity in the process. I was not willing to do that when difficult decisions had to be made. From the closing of schools (two in Whittier and two in Woodland) to unpopular budget reductions, the best interest of students and the district guided my decision recommendations.

- *Political astuteness.* Superintendents who cannot deal with the politics of the job would be well served to consider a career move. Superintendency has been cited as being one of the most political jobs around. Every decision made appears to have some political ramification or consequence in today's world. I like politics, and navigated the shark-ridden waters of the job on a daily basis. Whenever an issue arose (e.g., more than 100-foot poles for a wireless system), the array of consequences would flash before my eyes. That one almost caused me to stop breathing. Then time would be devoted to exploring the pros and cons and developing strategies to offset the negatives if that were the desired direction.

Lindsey: *Describe some of the important qualities for women (women of color) leaders in education.*

Robles: Women leaders bring a new dimension to leadership through their natural collaborative style, great listening skills, empathy and willingness to see both sides of an issue, and work toward a win-win solution. Not to say that men don't do that, but women leaders seem to do it more naturally. Once women leaders take on an administrative position, they seem to stay longer in the position than men. I believe this "staying power" and willingness to stay for the long haul is more evident in women leaders despite other professional growth opportunities.

Franco: I believe it is important that women of color exhibit qualities such as these:

- Competence
- Outstanding oral and written skills
- Ability to relate to *all* races, ethnicities, social and economic classes, and, in particular, the Anglo establishment

Ott: Women in leadership roles have a unique opportunity to move the achievement agenda for all children. I believe that women who have overcome barriers to achieve the title of leader represent the commitment to the success of all children. Having others follow your lead is a great honor, and I believe that women must use the opportunity wisely. Women can have a powerful impact on classrooms, schools, and districts by bringing diverse groups together to work on ensuring the academic success of students of all ethnic backgrounds.

Women are good listeners, and they generally do not let their egos get in the way of what is best for schools, children, and the community. Women tend to be collaborative, and this quality allows them to bring everyone together around a common agenda.

Graham: *What are some of the difficulties you have experienced as a woman of color administrator?*

Franco: In reflecting on the difficulties I encountered as a woman of color, the following stand out for me:

- *Had to work twice as hard.* I noticed over time that I was appearing at numerous events, whereas other colleagues would make occasional appearances. I had to go above and beyond in bringing positive recognition to my school district. I believe that working twice as hard and being in a constant pursuit of excellence characterizes my entire career.

- *Experienced professional jealousy.* When asked to assume a key leadership role in a professional organization, I encountered remarks that can be construed to be of a jealous nature. No overt action was taken; however, it was readily obvious that another individual wanted my position.

- *Encountered unsupportive (female and male) supervisors.* In several instances, attempts were made by a supervisor to discourage my seeking other promotional opportunities. My time frame for advancement was delayed; however, persistence on my part and assistance from other mentors ameliorated this situation. Ultimately, I was successful, but I would have experienced more rapid advancement had there not been this level of obstruction.

- *Increases in the number of women in administration have been threatening in and of itself; adding color to it is an additional complexity.* I am aware of cases where women of color have been hired into administrative positions where there was definite resentment by white males in the organization. Some women survived it, and some did not. Some, I believe, were purposely set up to fail. I personally encountered the resentment situation, and, unlike a number of the cases observed, it did not result in a failure on my part. These examples highlight the particular importance for women of color to carefully assess the districts and positions for which they are applying. No good ever came out of being set up for failure, and, if one looks closely, the clues are there.

- *Saw, in the end, that it has been an asset for me.* The difficulties and challenges I faced definitely made me a stronger person, honed my survival skills, and gave me insights in to the political machinations for working in the educational administrative arena. In today's climate, it is not for the faint of heart. The challenge is not only to survive but to succeed.

Ott: At times, I found that others wanted to define me as a Latina rather than a qualified administrator. I was proud to be Latino, but I wanted to be viewed as a leader who had succeeded based on merit. In the 1970s and 1980s, traditional leaders would often say that you got your job because you are Latino. I got my job because

I worked hard and was competent, and this type of stereotyping was offensive to me and demeaning of the hard work of others like me. It always surprises me when comments are made about increased numbers of people of color at the leadership level. Few complaints occurred when district leaders were predominately represented by white individuals; however, when too many people of color advance to that level, questions surface regarding the shift in leadership.

My personal passion for helping English learners almost limited my access to the superintendency. Expertise in language acquisition should have defined me as a leader for all children, yet it was viewed as my entire expertise. I always caution women of color to not allow themselves to be defined by a single agenda.

Robles: Some people have underestimated me, and had low expectations of my work. That more than anything has annoyed me. When I accomplished something, some people seem to be surprised, as if I, a Latina, could not do it. This reaction has made me angry at times, but it has also energized me to do more and prove them wrong.

Lindsey: *How do women become identified with being in charge, without being identified with negative or unfeminine ways?*

Ott: Women must not hesitate to show their strength in leadership roles. Women should know their personal compass well so that they are consistent in their focus and clearly articulate their passion for creating successful educational environments for all children. Others look for consistency in the behavior of their leaders, and not being clear about what you stand for is one of the reasons that others will not follow. It is better to have disagreement with your priorities than to be someone who wavers in her beliefs.

Leaders must respect the culture in which they work, building on what is in place. Women are uniquely qualified to be bridge builders because they tend to nurture change rather than forcing others to move to a new way of doing things. Top-down leadership can be viewed as disrespectful, and women who are in charge tend to understand the need to bring people together in consensus for long-term success. A woman should be clear that her qualities as a woman are assets, and it is not necessary to behave like a male to be viewed as a strong leader.

Robles: You just lead. I don't think you can worry about how you will be identified or you will be stuck and not move forward. People will always have an opinion about you, whether that opinion is based on facts. As a leader, you must be who you are and be authentic. As for being feminine, there is nothing wrong with being who you are and still be in charge. Everyone's unique personalities and qualities will determine their success.

Franco: This is an interesting point. Obviously, women need to learn to play with the "big boys," but I don't interpret this as acting like them. That being said, I believe that both men and women in leadership roles portray themselves in distinct ways:

- Conducting business in a conservative and serious manner
- Being viewed as a business leader, in charge of a million-dollar operation
- Dressing appropriately for the position (e.g., business attire, dark suits)

I enjoyed wearing scarves, and they became a signature item for me over the years. I never wore nail polish; however, many other women leaders did. Personally, I saw it as a distraction to how I wanted to be perceived. My stance was a no-nonsense approach.

The issue of negative perceptions of women being in charge will be there as long as there is a dearth of women in top CEO positions. This has been a hard wheel to turn, and it continues to move very slowly. The logical interpretation is that women are not viewed as being able to run a major business; consequently, men continue to be named to those positions. When a woman does break through a glass ceiling, extreme scrutiny follows. Her every move and word comes under the microscope. I recall observing some of the male leaders, as I moved through the administrative chairs, and they were tough negotiators. The female role models, while nurturing, were tough also. In retrospect, while I might have come across a bit hard lined, that was counter to who I really was. Lessons learned: To the point of femininity, I have learned that being a strong leader did not mean I had to be unfriendly, and being warm and approachable did not need to signify weakness. Those lessons did not come easily, and it would have been good if a mentor had shared that with me early in my administrative career.

Graham: *In what ways are the issues surrounding authority similar for a male and female leader, specifically women of color?*

Robles: Anyone in authority will have issues around control and power or how we use the position. It is up to the leader, male or female, to understand that real authority comes when you give it away, and it ensures that everyone in your organization feels ownership and responsibility for the success of the organization. I don't see it different for women of color—only that we are always in a fishbowl. We will often be the first Latina in the position, and others will see us as representing all women of color, so the issue is our success determines the access women have into leadership roles.

Franco: The professional failures of women of color in the past two decades, in particular, colored (pardon the pun) how we were and are viewed. I recall being told if a Latina had failed in a superintendent role in a school district that I was interested in, that would not be the best place for me to go because of perceptions. I would ask, "Why should that be the case?" More recently, that conversation has involved both men and women of color in the same breath.

Superintendents are hired by boards of education, a group of individuals with their own backgrounds of views, opinions, and prejudices. There are boards who collectively and individually do not have confidence in a woman of color. Some have heard something negative about a former superintendent of color from a nearby school district. In some cases, the most damning are arrogant male board members, white and those of color, who have problems taking recommendations from a female superintendent of color. Their upbringing does not allow for women to rise to a position of authority. Unfortunately, boards with this mentality are not a match for an aspiring woman leader of color.

The lesson learned here is to do one's homework regarding the board members. A heartening note is that the previously mentioned description does not represent all board members, male or female. A great deal of education on this topic needs to be conducted with all board members, but in particular, with those in minority affiliations. One important way to overcome this barrier is the growth of our reputations as successful educational leaders, who just happen to be of color.

Ott: Male and female leaders share a common goal—to improve the educational outcomes for all children. How males and females approach moving toward this goal reflects their personal passions and, what I call, inner moral compasses. Leaders sacrifice on a personal level to be allowed to lead others. Women have the traditional challenges of balancing personal and professional lives, sustaining marriage and family, as they work long and arduous hours advancing their careers. Males have moved closer to the middle regarding family, yet they are viewed as being able to have a leadership role without family being viewed as a challenge. Societal values related to the role of women in leadership are changing; however, I find that the question of balance in one's personal life is one of the most frequently asked questions when I talk to women aspiring to become educational leaders.

Males and females must both make the tough calls and be willing to remain in the debate when it relates to students and their success. In this way, authority is similar and carries the same burden of responsibility. Both males and females are held accountable for outcomes. Success is a hard fact, and women and men are equally measured by data. The story of how success is achieved is the richer story, yet the public's desire for quick fixes only looks at data. Males and females face the same harsh criticism and challenge of leading in increasingly demanding times. I believe that the conversations that are taking place around educational reform must bring male and female leaders together to share best practice and to support one another in climbing the achievement-gap hill.

Lessons Learned From Our Careers

Themes have emerged as lessons during our careers to inform our approaches to school leadership from the beginning as teacher leaders to our current roles as superintendents. From our careers, two themes from our early lives have been reinforced and two new themes have emerged:

Family is important. Family continues to be important. Our immediate families expand to include husbands and their families. Two of our husbands have spent time in the education field, and one is not an educator, and the three spouses are similar in their support for our careers.

Culture is central to how we define ourselves. We recognize the importance of how ethnicity and gender as culture are viewed and experienced by those who have hindered or facilitated our careers. We also recognize the importance of culture in how educators view and regard students in our schools. Culture is of innermost importance in our service to our students and their communities.

Multiple mentors are indispensable. Mentoring comes in different directions and from different sources. Mentoring is within cultures and across cultural boundaries. Mentoring from other women and Latino/as has been instrumental in navigating into schools and districts where we were among the first women and first Latino/as. Similarly, cross-cultural mentoring from men or women from other racial, ethnic groups has helped us learn organizational cultures and overcome institutional barriers to discrimination.

Tenacity and perseverance are important to establishing and demonstrating commitment to our vision of what education can be for all students. Without a doubt, our early experiences with discrimination motivated us to seek equitable educational opportunities and outcomes for our students.

Lessons learned continues our journey of sharing our stories with you in the context of the Tools of Cultural Proficiency. Chapter 5 provides an analysis of our stories and lessons that have emerged framed with the Barriers to Cultural Proficiency juxtaposed against the Guiding Principles of Cultural Proficiency. Chapter 6 continues the analysis of our stories and the themes that have emerged using a Cultural Proficiency Leadership Rubric, which has the Cultural Proficiency Continuum and the Essential Elements of Cultural Competence as the two axes of the rubric.

Reflection

Now turn your attention to your career. With little doubt as you were reading about us, at times, you thought about the people and events that have shaped your story. In the space provided, reflect on your career—early leadership experiences, mentors who guided your development, and opportunities and challenges that you encountered in the communities you have served. You will find these recollections informative, as you understand and become increasingly intentional in your approach to leading schools today.

5

Lessons Learned

Acknowledging Barriers, Recognizing Cultural Assets

A leader is someone with the power to project either shadow or light onto some part of the world and onto the lives of the people who dwell there.

Parker Palmer (2000, p. 78)

Our lifetime and career experiences have helped us identify *leadership lessons learned*. In preparing this book, we realized the extent to which our cultural assets were instrumental in overcoming many of the barriers we faced in our formative years. We also realized how these cultural assets have surfaced throughout our careers. Two important points continue to evolve for us:

- Barriers that impede social and academic progress for women and people of color have led to leadership lessons learned that have fueled our dedication to serving equitably the academic and social needs of all students. Our experience as teachers and administrators has been to recognize and surmount barriers to our careers and, simultaneously, to confront barriers that impede the education of children and youth in schools and districts where we have served.

- Similarly, we have an understanding and appreciation for our cultural assets that have led to leadership lessons learned in challenging and overcoming barriers in our lives and careers that support our dedication for all students learning at high levels. The Guiding Principles of Cultural Proficiency, though not known to us expressly early in our careers, have been embedded in our core values as educators committed to making a difference for all students.

Purpose of Chapters 5 and 6

Chapters 5 and 6 chronicle how we used the four Tools of Cultural Proficiency to analyze our autobiographies and the transcripts from our interviews with Randy and Stephanie to surface our lessons learned themes. With the Tools of Cultural Proficiency in mind, this chapter is devoted to the following:

- Describing barriers we have experienced and observed that impede cultural proficiency
- Describing how the Guiding Principles serve as core values for our personal, professional, and organizational values and behavior

To complement this chapter, Chapter 6 presents the Cultural Proficiency Continuum and Essential Elements in a rubric format designed to describe how we have engaged in personal behavior and organizational policies and practices to more effectively serve all students.

Our personal and professional experiences discussed in Chapters 3 and 4 are the basis in this chapter to inform you, as nonformal and formal school leaders of your schools. We are learning about forces that either block (Barriers) or facilitate (Guiding Principles) student achievement. Our life experiences have entailed using our cultural assets to face and overcome barriers in our lives. From our childhoods to the early stages of our careers, we now realize that we had core values to guide our work as teachers, principals, and superintendents to serve the academic and social needs of all students.

Our Process

As we finished the first drafts of our autobiographies and began to discuss our responses to the questions posed in Chapter 3 and 4, we read and reread our autobiographies and the interview transcripts with particular attention to identifying Barriers and Guiding Principles described by Lindsey, Nuri Robins, and Terrell (2009). Acknowledging the barriers in our lives and early careers provided lessons learned in how our cultural assets prepared us to deal with obstacles in our careers as superintendents. Our experiences witnessing how family members confronted discrimination and how we responded to differential treatment because of our ethnicity as students has provided us with tactics and strategies that continue to serve us as superintendents. These important life lessons do not appear in university leadership preparation programs.

Barriers Versus Cultural Assets: The Tension of Change

It does not take a veteran educator to acknowledge that change is not easy. We have found implementing new practices in schools very difficult and often made more difficult when issues of ethnic and racial culture are embedded in change processes. In Chapter 1, we described the national context of a society shifting from being based in agriculture to industry and, now, in technology while undergoing significant demographic, cultural changes and shifts. Change is not easy. However, what we have learned is change is inevitable and natural. When properly understood and implemented, the change process can be led in ways that benefit all learners in our schools.

Leaders must be able to see the barriers and impediments to creating new conditions for teaching and learning while tenaciously fostering practices that benefit all students, schools, and districts. The Conceptual Framework of Cultural Proficiency is a mental model for managing change that we use to understand and tell our stories in ways that may inform you as you continue your journey to increased effectiveness as a leader (Lindsey, Nuri Robins, Terrell, 2009; Senge et al., 2000).

The Conceptual Framework as a Guide

Many school policies and practices reflect societal barriers; therefore, we use the conceptual framework to share how our cultural assets form the basis for core values that guide us as educational leaders. Recognizing and understanding the tension that exists for people and schools in barriers versus assets prepares you to better serve the students in your classroom, school, and district.

Table 5.1 presents the Conceptual Framework of Cultural Proficiency and shows the four Tools of Cultural Proficiency and the relationship of the tools to one another. Begin by reading Table 5.1 from the bottom up. Yes, we know that it is counterintuitive way for many of us to read, but after all, this is a cultural experience.

As you now know, this chapter describes two Tools of Cultural Proficiency—the Barriers to Cultural Proficiency and the Guiding Principles (e.g., core values) of Cultural Proficiency. Knowing the Barriers provides an understanding of how to overcome resistance to change within one's self and in our schools. The Guiding Principles serve as core values to meet the needs of populations not historically well served by our schools. Please note the Zone of Ethical Tension between the Barriers and the Guiding Principles, as it is the pivot point where educators have stark choices:

- We choose to be a victim of social forces and to believe in either cultural deficit theory or, every bit as damaging, the intractability of systemic oppression.
- We choose to believe in our capacity to be effective in cross-cultural interactions.

In Chapter 6, we discuss the remaining two tools of Cultural Proficiency—the Cultural Proficiency Continuum and Essential Elements of Cultural Proficiency. The Essential Elements are standards for personal and professional behavior as well as organizational policies and practices. Please note how the Guiding Principles as core values serve to inform the Essential Elements. When culture is viewed as an asset, educational successes can be crafted, both for ourselves as educators and for the communities we serve. Our experiences as educators have been devoted to the education of children, youth, and adults in all sectors of the communities we serve.

Table 5.1 The Conceptual Framework for Culturally Proficient Practices

The Five Essential Elements of Cultural Competence

Serve as standards for personal, professional values and behaviors, as well as organizational policies and practices:

- Assessing cultural knowledge
- Valuing diversity
- Managing the dynamics of difference
- Adapting to diversity
- Institutionalizing cultural knowledge

The Cultural Proficiency Continuum portrays people and organizations who possess the knowledge, skills, and moral bearing to distinguish among healthy and unhealthy practices as represented by different worldviews:

Unhealthy Practices	Differing Worldviews	*Healthy Practices*
• Cultural destructiveness • Cultural incapacity • Cultural blindness		• Cultural precompetence • Cultural competence • Cultural proficiency

Resolving the tension to do what is socially just within our diverse society leads people and organizations to view selves in terms Unhealthy and Healthy.

Barriers to Cultural Proficiency	E t h i c a l	**Guiding Principles of Cultural Proficiency**
Serve as personal, professional, and institutional impediments to moral and just service to a diverse society by • being resistant to change, • being unaware of the need to adapt, • not acknowledging systemic oppression, and • benefiting from a sense of privilege and entitlement.	T e n s i o n	*Provide a moral framework for conducting one's self and organization in an ethical fashion by believing the following:* • Culture is a predominant force in society. • People are served in varying degrees by the dominant culture. • People have individual and group identities. • Diversity within cultures is vast and significant. • Each cultural group has unique cultural needs. • The best of both worlds enhances the capacity of all. • The family, as defined by each culture, is the primary system of support in the education of children. • School systems must recognize that marginalized populations have to be at least bicultural and that this status creates a distinct set of issues to which the system must be equipped to respond. • Inherent in cross-cultural interactions are dynamics that must be acknowledged, adjusted to, and accepted.

Source: From *Cultural Proficiency: A Manual for School Leaders* (3rd ed., p. 60), by R. B. Lindsey, K. Nuri Robins, and R. D. Terrell, 2009, Thousand Oaks: Corwin. Copyright © 2009 by Randall B. Lindsey, Kikanza Nuri Robins, and Raymond D. Terrell. Reprinted with permission.

Leading Lessons: The Barriers

Our careers have been marked by both challenging and positive experiences that have contributed to what we call *leading lessons*. Leading lessons are the formative lessons one learns on the job that later, and upon reflection, have helped to inform our larger, more enduring lessons learned. In this section, we focus on how we have turned barriers into leading lessons. From Table 5.1, you learned there are barriers to culturally proficient attitudes, behaviors, policies, and practices that affect our daily lives and impact educational leaders' decisions (Cross, Bazron, Dennis, & Isaacs, 1989; Lindsey, Nuri Robins, & Terrell, 1999, 2003, 2009):

- Being resistant to change
- Being unaware of the need to adapt
- Not acknowledging systemic oppression
- Benefiting from a sense of privilege and entitlement

In the section that follows, you are provided illustrations of our experiences with the Barriers to Cultural Proficiency that occurred throughout our professional and personal lives. Following this section is a lesson learned part derived from this explication of our experiences with barriers to our academic advancement, as well as that of others. As you read our selections, be mindful of the barriers that you may have experienced or are experiencing as well as barriers that exist for students in your school.

Randy and Stephanie's composite discussion is drawn from questions specific to the Barriers and the Guiding Principles and from our autobiographies. The complete text of our responses to the questions and our autobiographies are in the Resources. At two junctures, you are provided the opportunity to reflect on our experiences as well as on your professional life and aspirations. A deep understanding of how the Guiding Principles serve as core values to meet and overcome personal and institutional barriers will guide your journey to becoming Culturally Proficient.

Lindsey: *What are some personal or institutional examples of resistance to change that you have experienced in your careers?*

Franco: One of the hardest barriers for me was being asked in my second year of teaching, "Why would a nice, young woman like you want to be a principal?" Another example during my career was that as the number of women administrators increased, it was threatening to many men, and adding color was an additional complexity.

Ott: The emerging awareness, while in college, of low expectations held for students in K–12 schools for Latinos was a time of personal reflection on why others resist change. During my first superintendency, in an elementary school district, I met resistance from the high school district to allow a unification effort to move forward.

Robles: While at the University of Southern California (USC), it was difficult being treated as if we should feel honored just to be there. Later in my career, having my credentials (e.g., PhD and demonstrated competence) trumped by the perception of color and gender being more important was also a barrier.

Graham: *In reflecting on your career, what are some experiences where your fellow educators or institutions were not aware of the need to adapt to having women or Latinas as colleagues or administrators? Do you have illustrations of situations where fellow educators or schools failed to see that they should adapt to the students they have, in contrast to the students who used to attend their school or the students they wished they had?*

Ott: As a teacher, my principal was cautious in allowing me to speak Spanish with students during preparation for Cinco de Mayo event. When I was serving in my second assignment as principal, I was offered a promotion by senior-level administrators who did not recognize my school's need for stable, long-term leadership.

Robles: In one of my first district office positions, the state was experiencing a budget crisis, which revealed the dysfunction of the district and its inability to respond to very real needs of the changing demographics of students. The district used the excuse of a budget crisis to eliminate programs that served the students with greatest needs. Then, I moved to my second superintendents' position and learned that English learner students were not included in the initial student data accountability system, again, despite the changing demographics in our district and the state.

Franco: Early in my career, I learned that women of color had to be viewed as competent leaders. Later, when applying for a master's degree program in school administration, I was told to pursue another major.

Lindsey: *Are there instances in your career where you have experienced or witnessed systemic oppression, such as racism or sexism?*

Franco: Two experiences come to mind easily. First, the professional jealousy I experienced in displaying interest in leadership roles, and now, believing a negative perception of women administrators will remain as long as there is a dearth of women in top CEO positions.

Ott: It was very clear to me, as early as elementary school, when teachers would ask me why I didn't look like my (fair-complexioned) mother that I was perceived as different. Also, at that time in my life, I witnessed my father, an army veteran, being the object of racial epithets hurled by young, white males. I remember distinctly, as a young teacher, being disturbed by so many Latino students being labeled as "special education."

Robles: I have two vivid recollections as a child. First, I felt rejection from my teacher who commented on my dark skin color and, then, to have my family display bias toward my African American friend. As an administrator, it is disquieting to learn how often resources are disproportionately apportioned to wealthy communities within school districts.

Graham: *Following on Randy's question, have you experienced or witnessed occasions when fellow educators appeared to benefit from systemic oppression and, maybe, were completely unaware of such benefits?*

Ott: Unfortunately, many illustrations eat at the fabric of our schools. My first real understanding of entitlement came as a principal in seeing how often ineffective administrators were shuffled to schools where the community was not likely to protest or even know of their ineffectiveness. Most recently, I have witnessed parents use public schools for personal preference under the guise of parental choice. The choice was more about moving to a more homogeneous school district.

Robles: As a young administrator, I was visiting the local high school to help a young English learner student enroll. When approached by the assistant principal, she would not even listen to my concerns saying she doesn't "deal with aides." I realized that unless you have status you will not be heard. Later, as a superintendent, I was in a district where some community members and staff resisted separating religion from public school issues.

Franco: From the earliest stages of my career, I saw that as the number of women increased in administration it was threatening to many men. Skin color was an additional complexity.

Leadership Lesson Learned Derived From Barriers

Using the Tools of Cultural Proficiency to analyze our responses to the 13 questions and our autobiographies has been meaningful to the study of our careers. Specifically, using the Barriers to Cultural Proficiency as a lens added depth to our understanding of our tenacity and perseverance. Please note that the Barriers are not impenetrable, but they are surmountable only when recognized, confronted, and acknowledged. As school leaders, we have learned the importance of correctly identifying organizational and educator impediments to student learning.

Tenacity and perseverance are important to overcoming barriers in establishing and demonstrating commitment to our vision of what education can be for all students. Without a doubt, our early experiences with discrimination have motivated us to seek equitable educational opportunities and outcomes for our students.

- Life brings challenges and our role as school leaders is to help our colleagues see challenges facing our students and communities.
- Life may not be fair, but we are uniquely positioned to help our students gain the knowledge and skills to have an opportunity to craft their futures.

Reflection

Take a couple of minutes and think about barriers to student access and academic advancement. What is your reaction to the barriers concept? Do you recognize any barriers to your effectiveness across cultural lines? Do you recognize any ways in which you might be unaware of barriers for your students? What might be institutional barriers that exist for students in your school? Please use the space provided to record your thinking.

_____

_____

_____

_____

Leading Lessons: Cultural Assets

Attitudes and behaviors that esteem culture are grounded in core values that contribute directly to constructive leading lessons. In this section, illustrations link core values and leaders' attitudes and behaviors. From Table 5.1, you know Guiding Principles serve as core values for people and organizations who hold culture as an asset and who are committed to being successful in cross-cultural interactions, both as a person and as a member of an organization:

- Culture is a predominant force in society.
- People are served in varying degrees by the dominant society.
- People have individual and group identities.
- Diversity within cultures is vast and significant.
- Each cultural group has unique cultural needs.
- The best of both worlds enhances the capacity of all.
- The family, as defined by each culture, is the primary system of support in the education of children.
- School systems must recognize that marginalized populations have to be at least bicultural and that this status creates a distinct set of issues to which the system must be equipped to respond.
- Inherent in cross-cultural interactions are dynamics that must be acknowledged, adjusted to, and accepted.

In this section, we provide illustrations of our experiences consistent with the Guiding Principles of Cultural Proficiency. We have selected events that occurred throughout our professional and personal lives as well as lessons learned from our developing core values consistent with the Guiding Principles that have fostered our and others' academic advancement. As you read our selections, think of your core values and the school's core values that support all students in your school. Pay particular attention to the centrality of culture in each selection.

Lindsey: *Given your intimate knowledge of the Guiding Principles of Cultural Proficiency, I am interested to know brief examples or illustrations of the manner in which you have experienced or witnessed benefits from culture being valued in schools and society. I will present each guiding principle and would like for each of you to provide brief examples or illustrations.*

Culture is a predominant force in society.

Franco: Early in life, I was raised in a supportive, multiethnic community.

Ott: I had a supportive mother and grandmother in Germany, and then I was immersed into a proud, Mexican family. As a teacher, I used my fear of not feeling worthy as motivation and passion in service to students from disadvantaged backgrounds.

Robles: I learned independence by being reared in single-parent home. I was also able to experience living with an extended family that was proud of their cultural heritage.

People are served in varying degrees by the dominant society.

Ott: I was viewed by my high school teachers as talented, and I was expected to go to college. By this point in my education, I had learned "the rules," and I navigated my way to college. I became a Title VII bilingual teacher, which increased my leadership experience.

Robles: As superintendent, I was willing to stand for integrity when board members interfered in principal appointment. Bringing the Annenberg grant to the district provided professional development in support of closing achievement disparities. I was also the first Latina in three superintendent positions.

Franco: In my first superintendency, I was hired by an all-white board because of my competence. Being Latina was icing. In that district, we used categorical money to provide historically underserved students with educational opportunities that extended beyond the normal school experiences.

People have individual and group identities.

Robles: I value being respected and being respectful of differing opinions and voices. Everyone has something to contribute.

Franco: I realized that to be a leader it is not necessary to emulate men. To be viewed as a business leader, I conduct myself in a conservative and serious manner.

Ott: I work to meet the needs of students through differentiated instruction.

Diversity within cultures is vast and significant.

Franco: I observed successful women and became involved in women's professional organizations.

Ott: I am driven by the passion for serving needs of students from impoverished backgrounds. I have devoted my career to helping teachers acquire expertise in closing the achievement gap and helping students learn English.

Robles: One of my first tasks as the new superintendent of Salt Lake City schools was to understand the local context (e.g., culture).

Each cultural group has unique cultural needs.

Ott: I attended Mount St. Mary's, which is committed to minority women, especially Latinas.

Robles: I demonstrated commitment to equal access to the Gay Straight Alliance while I was the superintendent of Salt Lake City Schools.

Franco: Two examples come to mind. As indicated previously, in my first district we provided learning opportunities for students that extended beyond the traditional school day. Another example is mentoring women of color who were enrolled in the superintendents' academy.

The best of both worlds enhances the capacity of all.

Robles: Being in different schools in elementary school and learning how to develop friendships and relationships with many different groups of students and neighborhoods was a great experience for me. It taught me to be flexible, adaptable, and a risk taker.

Franco: I did my homework to learn about board members' perceived views and to develop my reputation as an educational leader, independent of gender or ethnicity.

Ott: I had a supportive mother and grandmother in Germany, and then I was immersed into a proud, Mexican family.

> *The family, as defined by each culture, is the*
> *primary system of support in the education of children.*

Franco: I served as a role model for inviting all members of the community to be involved in school and school-related activities.

Ott: I was involved in a broad-based group of constituents that develop the Rowland Strategic Plan.

Robles: I demonstrated commitment to equal access in Gay Straight Alliance issues, and instituted strong parent programs in Los Angeles County to empower parents to demand the best for their children.

> *School systems must recognize that marginalized populations have*
> *to be at least bicultural and that this status creates a distinct set of*
> *issues to which the system must be equipped to respond.*

Ott: In 1993, I received a call from another mentor, Darline P. Robles, encouraging me to apply for the superintendent vacancy in the Little Lake City School District (California). My first reaction to this encouragement was that I could not see myself as a superintendent, and I certainly did not see myself leaving my career in LAUSD. In retrospect, I realize that my background showed up as fear of not being worthy. When children grow up in poverty, they carry self-doubt about their worthiness. Although I had a successful career, my past has always influenced my life. This self-awareness keeps my passion for helping children alive and strong.

Robles: When I arrived in Salt Lake City, the city was experiencing many demographic changes: an increase in the number of English learners, more students from different ethnic groups, and more students living in poverty. My goal was to make this data transparent.

If we did not share this data, our public would not be able to understand the challenges in our schools. We began to disaggregate data by all subgroups. I also had to confront a state data system that did not include English learners in the system. To implement a reform agenda, we decided to apply for funds from the Annenberg Foundation. We were pleased to be awarded a $12 million grant. This was the impetus to make major changes in our programs to meet the diverse needs of our students. Over time, our public began to understand the term "equity" as it pertained to our students.

Franco: I have always refused to settle for less than the highest expectations, especially as it applied to what we were doing for students and their families. When parents heard that I was going to see that their children had experiences and programs like those in higher-economic settings (e.g., Beverly Hills), they were ecstatic. It generated a tremendous amount of parental support for the schools.

> *Inherent in cross-cultural interactions are dynamics that must be acknowledged, adjusted to, and accepted.*

Robles: I was direct with the community about the negative behavior of some students and community members toward the students in Gay Straight Alliance and the likelihood of students being harmed. I am willing to be honest and direct.

Franco: I enjoyed expanding political awareness because of having board members' children and grandchildren in the school district.

Ott: My bilingual educator role opened doors to serving as translator at parent meetings to bridge understanding between the community and the school and supported classroom teachers with ESL students.

Leadership Lesson Learned Derived From the Guiding Principles

Culture is central to how we define ourselves. We recognize the importance of how ethnicity and gender as culture are viewed and experienced by those who have hindered or facilitated our careers. We also recognize the importance of culture in the context of how educators view and regard students in our schools. We find that guiding our educator colleagues to develop the willingness to embrace culture from an assets-based perspective is of innermost importance in our service to our students and their communities.

Reflection

In the introduction to this section, we invited you to think about your and your school's core values. Also, we asked that you pay attention to the centrality of culture in the Guiding Principles. How do you react to the concept of culture? In what ways do your core values and those of your school embrace culture? Please use the space provided to describe how a stranger to your school would recognize your commitment to culture as an asset.

_____

_____

_____

_____

Chapter 6 presents the remaining Tools of Cultural Proficiency, the Cultural Proficiency Continuum, and the Essential Elements arrayed into a leadership rubric. This chapter has provided an understanding of forces that impede or facilitate success in schools, namely, Barriers and Guiding Principles. Chapter 6 provides detailed descriptions of individual values and behaviors and organizational policies and practices that are based within the Barriers or the Guiding Principles. As an educational leader, you will find the illustrations most helpful.

6

Lessons Learned

Cultural Assets Inform Actions

*History will have to record that the greatest tragedy of this period
. . . was not the strident clamor of the bad people, but the appall-
ing silence of the good people.*

Martin Luther King, Jr. (Anderson, 2007, p. 37)

This chapter summarizes our personal and professional experiences discussed in Chapters 3 and 4 to inform you, as formal and
nonformal school leaders of our schools, of the *leadership lessons
learned* and the manner in which our cultural assets have shaped our
core values. In turn, from our core values, standards of practice
emerged to guide our personal and professional behavior as well as
the development and implementation of policies and practices within
our schools and school districts. Our standards of practice merge with
the Essential Elements of Cultural Proficiency and function as an
important tool for personal and organizational planning.

Leading Lessons in a Rubric

Once our leadership standards emerged from analysis of our responses
to the 13 questions and to our autobiographies, we turned to our

colleague Stephanie Graham to develop a leadership rubric. Stephanie's prior experience with development of cultural proficiency rubrics began when writing with coauthors (Lindsey, Graham, Westphal, Jr., & Jew, 2008) and with colleagues in the Los Angeles County Office of Education where they developed cultural proficiency rubrics appropriate to several content areas. Over several weeks, Stephanie developed drafts of the rubric, to which we responded, edits were made, and, as the final step, other authors of Cultural Proficiency books provided feedback to ensure consistency in application of operational definitions of the six points of the Cultural Proficiency Continuum and the Five Essential Elements.

Within each of the Essential Elements, Stephanie incorporated aspects from our responses to the 13 questions and biographical narratives to illustrate leadership behaviors and patterns. These illustrations from our narratives and autobiographies served to inform each Essential Element to function as leverage points that, in the hands of a skillful leader, can serve as a template for planning personal and organizational change.

Table 6.1 presents the Culturally Proficient Leadership Rubric. The descriptions under the first column are operational descriptions of the role of school leaders for each Essential Element to be used as leverage points for formative personal and organizational growth. Please use this guide for reading and interpreting Table 6.1, the Culturally Proficient Leadership Rubric:

- Note the rubric is comprised of rows and columns.
- Each of the rows is one of the five standards referred to as an Essential Element of Cultural Competence. The first column represents an operational definition of each Essential Element as a formative leverage point of change for school leaders and their schools/districts.
- There are seven columns. At the top of the first column is Essential Elements. Columns 2 through 6 are the phases of the Cultural Proficiency Continuum.
- As you read from Cultural Destructiveness to Cultural Competence for each of the five Essential Elements, you are viewing the Essential Elements as subleverage points in the progression of change for school leaders and their schools/districts.
- The sixth column is Cultural Competence. Each of the descriptors in that column describes one of the essential elements of cultural competence. The language is in active voice and describes actions that can be taken today in schools. It is at Cultural Competence that a standard is deemed "met" and is measurable.
- The seventh column is Cultural Proficiency. The description is future focused.

Table 6.1 Cultural Proficiency Leadership Rubric

Assessing Culture (One's Own and Others)	Informed by Barriers to Cultural Proficiency		
	Cultural Destructiveness	*Cultural Incapacity*	*Cultural Blindness*
The extent to which the leader uses personal experience to develop, maintain, and provoke a moral imperative (passion, knowledge, wisdom, diligence, and courage) for making positive changes that benefit underserved stakeholders in schools and in the community.	Leaders rely on a narrow definition of "American culture" to develop and justify policies and procedures and resource allocation to those they believe are more entitled or capable than others to receive those resources while denying or restricting resources to those deemed "unworthy" or incapable of achieving success in America.	Leaders tolerate diversity in schools but believe that the perspectives and attributes of the dominant culture are superior to those of other cultures. This belief justifies policies and practices that maintain the status quo and benefit those that reflect the attributes of the dominant culture while limiting the leader's motivation and resolve to make changes to benefit underserved stakeholders.	Leaders demonstrate managerial competence by supporting and being supported by agency policies and practices that support a culture of continuous improvement for all students regardless of their cultural backgrounds and experiences. Evidence of effectiveness is limited to single measures, such as agency-sanctioned standardized test scores, which reinforce the belief that "some students just do better than others."
The extent to which the leader perceives aspects of culture as assets and strengths (not deficits) to harness and optimize for effective teaching, learning, and leadership.	Leaders believe that displays of culture are barriers to their progress and the progress of others. Hence, such displays are repressed, discouraged, disparaged, or punished.	Leaders disavow the influence that culture has on learning and/or one's professional actions. They promote assimilation to the dominant culture of society, school, or the organization, often downplaying or hiding aspects of culture, believing them to reflect negatively on one's leadership capacity and competence. Leaders promote programs that aim to	Leaders believe that culturally defined aspects such as "motivation," "talent," and "diligence," not culture, influence learning, performance, and success. Focusing on aspects of culture is an unnecessary distraction or excuse for not learning or not being successful and may deter one's advancement or promotion.

Informed by Guiding Principles of Cultural Proficiency		
Cultural Precompetence	*Cultural Competence*	*Cultural Proficiency*
Leaders are compassionate, caring, diligent professionals whose backgrounds compel a narrow focus on serving a particular cultural group, often the same culture as the leaders'. Such a focus may limit the leaders' cultural capacity to advocate for all underserved students and reinforce a belief that minority leaders are more capable of developing relationships with and addressing the needs of minority stakeholders.	Leaders are compassionate, diligent, and skilled professionals whose experiences have led to a profound understanding of long-term, systemic educational inequity. This understanding compels a relentless, fervent professional and personal commitment to challenge and break down barriers to educational access, opportunity, and success and close gaps for historically underserved stakeholders.	Leaders are compassionate, diligent, and transformational professionals who understand that inequity in school is a microcosm of inequities in society. Such understanding compels a relentless commitment to educating all stakeholders about educational and social injustice, while also breaking down barriers to success for historically underserved stakeholders.
Leaders support programs, scholarships, networks, sponsorships, recruiting, hiring, promoting, and allocating resources for one or more cultural groups but such resources may be single or short-term opportunities intended to ensure success for stakeholders who need on-going support to navigate next steps toward success.	Leaders proudly assert their culture and culturally induced core values of courage, persistence, resiliency, risk taking, and self-determination while seeking and providing nurturing and supportive relationships, stewardship, and mentoring of other minority leaders and advocating for recruiting, hiring, and promoting other minority leaders with the passion and capacity for closing equity gaps for underserved stakeholders.	Leaders from both minority and majority cultures understand how cultural identity (membership and status) can influence learning and success. Leaders embrace and leverage attributes of their and others' cultures as assets to achieve organizational goals while accelerating progress and closing gaps for historically underserved groups in schools and in the community.

(Continued)

Table 6.1 (Continued)

Assessing Culture (One's Own and Others)	Informed by Barriers to Cultural Proficiency		
	Cultural Destructiveness	*Cultural Incapacity*	*Cultural Blindness*
		remediate or assimilate underperforming students, limiting student access and progress, and often exacerbating access and achievement gaps.	

	Informed by Barriers to Cultural Proficiency		
Valuing Diversity	*Cultural Destructiveness*	*Cultural Incapacity*	*Cultural Blindness*
The extent to which the leader is aware of, values, learns about, supports, and promotes her culture and the culture of others.	Leaders are fearful or discouraged about or disparaged for promoting and demonstrating aspects of culture.	Leaders avoid making reference to their own or others' cultural perspectives and behaviors and assimilate to the expected roles of the organization. Leaders expect others, including community members and students, to assimilate to be successful in school and in society.	Leaders do not believe there is any value to understanding culture to enhance or promote staff, leader, or student performance and success.
The extent to which the leader seeks, respects, and values multiple diverse ideas, opinions, cultural perspectives, experiences, and styles to inform decisions for the good of the organization and the community.	Leaders promote/display dominant group values and behaviors, ignoring or excluding diverse perspectives and often making decisions that only benefit stakeholders from the dominant culture.	Leaders solicit input and participation from diverse community members to comply with agency or funding source requirements for participation and representation of diverse groups.	Leaders believe ones' education and experience has adequately informed her decisions and actions. Soliciting community input is a polite political distraction but yields little toward attaining one's leadership goals.

Informed by Guiding Principles of Cultural Proficiency		
Cultural Precompetence	*Cultural Competence*	*Cultural Proficiency*

Informed by Guiding Principles of Cultural Proficiency		
Cultural Precompetence	*Cultural Competence*	*Cultural Proficiency*
Leaders consider the cultural backgrounds of others when recruiting and hiring, and may have been hired because of their cultural background, supporting a belief that minority cultural group staff and leaders are more capable of understanding and addressing cultural minority stakeholder needs and issues.	Leaders understand the influence of culture on learning, teaching, and leading, and promote culture as an asset to performance and success.	Leaders promote cultural pluralism as a way of meeting the needs of all stakeholders, not only those with the loudest voice, and to promote distribution of political, societal, and economic power among diverse groups, not just among an entitled electorate.
Leaders assign others or are assigned to work with stakeholders from their culture(s) because it is believed that being from a particular cultural group can better foster understanding, trust, and buy-in into the goals, policies, and decisions of the organization.	Leaders promote and model learning about the community in authentic ways for all stakeholders so that the specific cultural perspectives, issues, and needs of all community groups can be better understood and addressed by all in the organization.	Leaders promote community building to exchange data and information to collaborate on common goals among disparate constituents and share resources for closing educational, societal, and economic gaps.

(Continued)

Table 6.1 (Continued)

Managing the Dynamics of Difference	Informed by Barriers to Cultural Proficiency		
	Cultural Destructiveness	*Cultural Incapacity*	*Cultural Blindness*
The extent to which the leader solicits diverse points of view, opinions, learning, communication, and leadership styles to promote flexibility in meeting organizational goals and to make decisions, which reflect stakeholder issues.	Leaders make unilateral, authoritarian decisions with little or no input about stakeholder needs. Leaders may solicit particular perspectives to justify decisions or to withhold or deny programs, services, or resources to some stakeholders. Leaders' inflexibility and adherence to the structures and styles of the dominant organizational culture discourage participation of diverse stakeholders leading to policies and practices that ignore or exclude their needs and issues.	Leaders may solicit input from diverse cultural groups, often only to comply with program regulations and not to incorporate diverse perspectives into decisions. Leaders attempting to manage the status quo and preserve tradition are not open to alternative ways to achieve goals and/or to meet the needs of diverse stakeholders. Hence, leaders make decisions or take action that misrepresents, disrespects, or trivializes the perspectives and issues of diverse stakeholders.	Leaders believe they are effective when they can prevent, mitigate, and avoid dissonance and conflict, especially conflict rising from diverse cultural perspectives. Few attempts are made to solicit diverse points of view, thereby reducing the opportunity for conflict and considerations of diverse perspectives. Leaders may facilitate consensus or bring multiple issues to a vote, often excluding diverse stakeholders' ideas and issues.
The extent to which the leader embraces risk to make decisions and take actions, which may not be popular with dominant cultures, anticipates criticism, persists in the face of criticism, inertia, barriers or reversals, and accepts personal and professional consequences advocating for underserved students and other stakeholders.	Leaders' ambiguity about who they are and why they are in the role results in passivity and conformity to low-level expectations and responsibility. Leaders lead without a moral purpose or imperative. In the face of conflict or criticism, leaders assert authority, withdraw from or totally ignore it.	Leaders from minority cultures are expected to maintain the status quo. Such leaders are professionally intimidated from taking risks or challenging the system. Innovation, creativity, and trailblazing are encouraged and rewarded for leaders from dominant group members to preserve a dominant cultural perspective in all leadership policies and practices.	Leaders believe it is organizationally expedient and encourage others to promote ideas and decisions that are popular and supported by the dominant or the majority groups, hence avoiding taking risks or being criticized for challenging the system.

Informed by Guiding Principles of Cultural Proficiency		
Cultural Precompetence	*Cultural Competence*	*Cultural Proficiency*
Leaders may consider input from majority stakeholder groups and/or one or few minority stakeholder groups depending on which stakeholders proactively assert their ideas and opinions. Leader may wrongly assume that stakeholders who do not come forward to make their needs known are satisfied with the status quo.	Leaders encourage diverse opinions and perspectives and facilitate conversations across cultures and viewpoints in productive, noncontentious and nonpolarizing ways. They engage in on-going dialogue between and among groups to help the organization develop a customer-service orientation and challenge the status quo by promoting organizational flexibility to meet diverse customer needs.	Leaders use conflict as a catalyst for dialogue to deepen personal, organizational, and community understanding about educational and societal injustice. Leaders use data to help stakeholders understand patterns of underperformance and underutilization of resources for some groups and to shift deficit thinking about diverse stakeholders to shared responsibility for better meeting their needs.
Leaders take calculated risks, perhaps in favor of a particular issue or demographic group but not consistently for all underserved stakeholders or for all issues that require advocacy from an organizational leader. Leaders avoid taking risks or being criticized if they perceive personal, professional, or political threat or negative consequences.	Leaders embrace risk, make decisions, and take action, which may not be popular with dominant cultures. They anticipate criticism; persist in the face of criticism, inertia, barriers, or reversals; and accept personal and professional consequences for their advocacy for underserved students and other stakeholders.	Leaders embrace risk and criticism as necessary on their leadership journey and on their quest for what is right and just. Because failure is not an option and professional goals and personal goals are the same, persistence and progress, however challenged or challenging, empower leaders as lifetime agents for equity and social justice.

(Continued)

Table 6.1 (Continued)

Adapting to Diversity	Informed by Barriers to Cultural Proficiency		
	Cultural Destructiveness	*Cultural Incapacity*	*Cultural Blindness*
The extent to which the leader facilitates an understanding about the truth of an organization's effectiveness in achieving equitable outcomes.	Leaders do not collect, share, or disaggregate data that shows patterns of performance for underserved groups. Leaders may misuse disaggregated data to reinforce deficit perspectives about some students/parents to justify withholding resources for some groups. Data is used to conceal or manipulate the truth.	Leaders use data to develop programs and services that focus on intervention or remediation but limit student access to further learning opportunities needed for educational success or post-school options. Data is used to obscure the truth and serve the organization's needs but not challenge its capacity to adapt to meet stakeholder needs.	Leaders primarily use norm-referenced test data to sort, select, and track students into programs. Improvement for all groups is the focus rather than closing data-informed gaps. Leaders believe that standardized test scores present an objective picture of the range of ability and the inevitable performance "curve" of diverse students.
The extent to which the leader (1) helps others understand the sources of assumptions that may obscure the truth about the organization's effectiveness and diminishes personal responsibility for achieving it and (2) builds capacity to transform the organization's ability to achieve outcomes for equity and justice.	Leaders do not use data to create an understanding of the school's effectiveness with specific populations nor do they use data to inform conversations and decisions. Prevailing assumptions and biases go unchallenged.	Leaders expect students and their parents to take advantage of existing school opportunities, which they believe, are effectively meeting the learning needs of underperforming students. Leaders and staff cannot be held responsible if students and parents do not participate in or complete such programs.	Leaders believe and promote that there are factors that influence student performance that are beyond the purview of the school. Therefore, there is only so much outcome data for which the school can and should accept responsibility.
The extent to which the leader manifests and develops in others a congruence between personal identity and purpose and vocational identity and purpose (leadership integrity).	Leaders' identities and actions are disconnected from the moral purpose of school, often leading to passivity, cynicism, and unethical or unjust leadership.	Leaders' identities and actions are congruent with a deficit perspective of diverse students and a well-intended vocational purpose to remediate and assimilate them "for their own good."	Leaders' identities and actions are congruent with a pedagogy for equality but not equity.

Informed by Guiding Principles of Cultural Proficiency		
Cultural Precompetence	*Cultural Competence*	*Cultural Proficiency*
Leaders may use/share data to highlight disproportionate outcomes and access to services. If they do, leaders may limit focus to one underperforming group over others or direct efforts at raising test scores without necessarily removing barriers to student learning.	Leaders use/share multiple sources of data that clarify disproportionate pattern over time for demographic groups. Leaders examine not only achievement data but also access and opportunity data to close gaps sooner rather than later when disparities show up in test-score data.	Leaders share data with other organizations to build understanding about cross-organizational effectiveness in meeting underserved stakeholders' needs. From this, leaders forge a cross-agency vision and commitment to sharing resources to build organizations that change people and their capacity to structure society for socially just ends.
Leaders respond to legal mandates to reduce disproportionality in specific programs or across the system. Often the measure of compliance is in the development of a plan or the delivery of a program or professional development but not in the reduction of the disproportionality.	Leaders challenge and encourage others to challenge policies, programs, and practices that correlate with disproportionate educational outcomes. They model and encourage risk taking and thinking outside of the box while holding themselves and others accountable for adapting, learning about, and applying new programs, structures, and practices that show evidence on multiple measures of narrowing educational gaps.	Leaders challenge and encourage others to challenge and dismantle legal mandates within and outside of the educational system that create barriers to success. Leaders form coalitions to lobby for legislations that ensures equitable access and outcomes for underserved stakeholders.
Leaders' identities and actions are congruent with helping or rescuing some students but not necessarily removing barriers to their success.	Leaders' identities and actions are congruent with pedagogy for educational equity (closing educational gaps).	Leaders' personal identities and purposes and vocational identities and purposes are integrated, one and the same, in their moral imperative for social justice.

(Continued)

Table 6.1 (Continued)

Institutionalizing Cultural Knowledge	Informed by Barriers to Cultural Proficiency		
	Cultural Destructiveness	*Cultural Incapacity*	*Cultural Blindness*
The extent to which the leader communicates openly, frequently, and effectively with all stakeholder groups and creates a culture of community collaboration and inclusive decision making focused on meeting the needs of underserved students and their parents/guardians.	Leaders avoid or resist communicating openly and effectively with all stakeholder groups believing some will not understand or are not worthy or capable of understanding the goals or policies of the organization. Decisions are made to intentionally thwart or exclude some voices that would require the organization to reallocate resources for underserved stakeholders.	Leaders communicate frequently with stakeholder groups with the loudest or most influential voices. Decisions are made unilaterally or by a few top school leaders, believing they know what is best for all groups, without seeking input from the communities that will be affected most by the decisions.	Leaders provide equal opportunities to give and receive communication from all groups but do not see the need to accommodate the context, environment, nuance, or language for the needs of some stakeholder groups. Leaders comply with decisions made by state/federal agencies and a few top administrators believing them to adequately benefit all stakeholders regardless of their cultural needs and styles.
The extent to which the leader promotes a persistent vision of education as the vehicle for closing societal gaps, makes a difference in the lives of others and creates support networks and structures for mentoring greatness in others.	Leaders use their position to acquire and assert authority, politicize education, and foment negative attitudes about some stakeholder groups in the school and community. Leaders use their authority to limit the power of others, grow their power, and use it to distort information and withhold resources for some groups. Leaders intimidate others to adopt and act on the leader's political values.	Leaders use their authority to ensure that others comply with state and district policies and procedures, believing them to adequately meet the educational needs of most students. Leaders ignore or attempt to remediate students with special needs, limiting their future educational options and success. Leaders seek success by assimilating to the dominant culture's standards for school leaders and expect others to do the same.	Leaders use their position to reinforce the meritocratic nature of school, being unaware or ignoring of disproportionate opportunity gaps experienced by some students. That some students succeed is evidence that the system is fair. Leaders see themselves as enforcers and maintainers of current educational policy not challengers of it.

Informed by Guiding Principles of Cultural Proficiency		
Cultural Precompetence	*Cultural Competence*	*Cultural Proficiency*
Leaders may translate communications for some stakeholder groups but not others. Leaders may accommodate communication strategies consistently to ensure effective cross-cultural communication for all groups. Leaders may seek input from cultural affinity groups but may not do so consistently for all cultural groups. Well-intentioned leaders may extrapolate information from a few members of one cultural group and assume it applies to all members of that group.	Leaders model effective and polished oral and written communication in the languages of the community while accommodating the context of the communication to meet stakeholder needs. Leaders seek input from multiple and varied stakeholder groups even if some groups do not assert their voices or perspectives. Decisions are made that consider all stakeholders' input, but the leader is not afraid to make a decision that primarily supports underserved stakeholders.	Leaders collaborate with community organizations to develop and use cross-cultural communication strategies to solicit stakeholder input, develop goals, and take action, which enhances multi-organizational credibility, trust, and effectiveness in meeting the needs of stakeholders. Leaders facilitate an understanding among all in the community that meeting the needs of the underserved contributes to the common good.
Leaders may use their position to make others aware of the equity gap for one or a few specific demographic groups. Often such leaders become outspoken advocates for a specific underperforming group, using their position to reallocate resources for such groups but not necessarily taking the risk to remove systemic barriers for some or all underserved groups.	Leaders use their position to inform stakeholders about the organization's effectiveness in meeting the needs of underserved stakeholders. Such leaders facilitate an understanding that transforming the system requires changing the service paradigm from equality to equity and replacing pedagogy for continuous improvement for all to pedagogy for closing gaps for the underserved.	Leaders inspire and are inspiring. They use their position to influence state and federal policy and resources to level the educational and societal playing field. Their wisdom and beneficence develops moral purpose in others, and empowers and rewards others' leadership successes. The fulfillment of contributing to the success of others grows the leader's capacity for enduring greatness.

Making Meaning of the Rubric

Now that you are familiar with the rubric, the following are a couple of activities you can use to deepen your understanding of the rubric and the role of school leader using the Essential Elements as leverage points for change. These activities are also highly effective professional development activities you can use with colleagues.

Adjectives and verbs. The first activity is to analyze the rubric to understand and be able to use the rubric as a diagnostic and planning tool. Follow these steps:

- Turn your attention to the first essential element, Assessing Cultural Knowledge.
- Study the *operational definition* of Assessing Cultural Knowledge in the first column. We refer to this definition as the *essence* of the essential element.
- Next, *read the examples* for Assessing Cultural Knowledge, beginning with Cultural Destructiveness and through Cultural Proficiency. You will have read six illustrations along the Continuum.
- Now, go back through the six illustrations and circle or highlight verbs and adjectives. What do you notice as you read from left to right? Record your observations and reactions.
- If conducting the activity with colleagues, compare and discuss your observations and reactions.
- Finally, perform the same analysis with the remaining four essential elements—Valuing Diversity, Managing the Dynamics of Difference, Adapting to Diversity, and Institutionalizing Cultural Knowledge.

After completing this activity, you will be equipped to use the rubric to diagnose and formatively develop your values and behaviors and your school's policies and practices. In Uses of the Rubric, we describe diagnostic applications of the rubric.

Reflection

Please use the space provided on the next page to record your observations and reactions to the adjectives and verbs activity. What did you see? What are your reactions? In what ways does the activity inform your understanding of the Essential Elements as standards for leadership practice?

_____

_____

_____

_____

Assumptions. This second activity engages you in analyzing the rubric by reading beneath the vertical columns, Informed by Barriers to Cultural Proficiency and Informed by the Guiding Principles of Cultural Proficiency. Follow these steps to guide your inquiry:

- Read the 15 cells headed by Informed by Barriers to Cultural Proficiency and note the assumptions embedded in the descriptions and illustrations.
- Summarize the assumptions for later reference.
- Now read the 15 cells headed by Informed by the Guiding Principles of Cultural Proficiency and note the assumptions embedded in the descriptions and illustrations.
- As with the previous step, summarize the assumptions.
- Examine the two sets of assumptions. In what ways do they compare and contrast? What are your observations and reactions to the assumptions you have uncovered?
- If conducting the activity with colleagues, compare and discuss your observations and reactions.

After completing these two activities, verbs and adjectives and assumptions, you are now prepared to use the rubric in your professional practice and with colleagues in service to your student population.

Reflection

In the space provided, please record your observations and reactions to the assumptions activity. What did you see? What are you reactions? In what ways does the activity inform your understanding of the Essential Elements as standards for leadership practice?

_____

_____

_____

_____

Uses of the Rubric. We have observed at least two uses of the rubric, one is inappropriate and the other is appropriate, useful, and productive.

- Inappropriate use of the rubric involves hearing a colleague make a comment or display a behavior that you can locate on the left side of the rubric and to inform them that you have demonstrable proof that they are Culturally Destructive, Culturally Incapacitous, or Culturally Blind. While it may be tempting to point out such behavior, it neither leads to good relations with colleagues nor does it lead to change that benefits students.
- Appropriate use of the rubric begins with the same analysis as in the previous illustration, but instead of making the other person the focus of your behavior, your focus is on what *you* do. For example, if the offending behavior is Culturally Destructive, you can use the rubric to examine options for what you say or do by reading the Culturally Precompetent, Culturally Competent, and Culturally Proficient illustrations.
- What we refer to as appropriate use of the rubric serves as an illustration of the inside-out approach of Cultural Proficiency.

The rubric provides formal and nonformal leaders a template for action. The rubric is not a stand-alone activity for school leaders, other educators, and their communities. The rubric is an action tool to assess progress toward clearly defined goals focused on improving student achievement. Effective use of the rubric as a leverage point for change depends on deep conversations that emerge from using the four Tools of Cultural Proficiency.

Leading Lesson Learned

Change is an intentional process. Personal and systemic change processes are constructed with recognition of the moral imperative of our work. Change processes value the students and communities we serve, are willing to engage those who agree and disagree with equanimity, embrace inequity as important information, and are inclusive and collaborative.

Reflection

In this chapter, we used a rubric to communicate behaviors that are unhealthy and healthy in pursuit of serving students from diverse cultural origins. You learned how the Barriers inform and reinforce Cultural Destructiveness, Cultural Incapacity, and Cultural Blindness. On the more positive side, you learned how Guiding Principles of Cultural Proficiency inform and support Cultural Precompetence, Cultural Competence, and Cultural Proficiency. Please use the space provided to describe what a stranger to your school or school district would witness that would demonstrate your school or school district's involvement with closing access and achievement gaps.

_____

_____

_____

_____

Chapter 7 summarizes our lessons learned and guides you in examining yourself as an educational leader committed to equitable outcomes for your students. You are also provided the opportunity to take a deep look at your school or school district and to develop, or improve, your equity leadership plan.

7

Developing Your Leadership for Equity Plan

Superintendency is more than an occupation, it is a calling.

Thelma Meléndez de Santa Ana (2008, p. 25)

Getting Centered

Educational leadership comes in many forms. We agree with Dr. Meléndez de Santa Ana that the superintendency is a calling, and we are sure she would agree with us that educational leadership in its many formal and nonformal versions is a calling for doing what is in the best interest of our students. To assist us in our work, we recorded our stories in this book and aligned them with the Tools of Cultural Proficiency for two purposes—as a personal record for each of us and to extend our mentoring of colleagues like you, the reader of this book. What does the term "calling" suggest to you? Please use the space provided to record your thoughts, images, and questions.

As we completed this manuscript, we learned of Margaret Grogan and Charol Shakeshaft's (2011) wonderful new book, *Women and Educational Leadership*. Their study yielded results that closely parallel our careers. For instance, their discussion about making meaning of leadership included the important observation that women's commitment to social justice, though not fully understood in all its ramifications, involved wanting to make things better (p. 90). Women's leadership for social justice may stem from our experiences as women being marginalized as school leaders and once inside the organization wanting to do whatever necessary to improve the lives of all students. The commitment to improving the academic lives of students is, assuredly, what has driven our dedication to leadership for equity.

Grogan and Shakeshaft (2011) identified five ways women lead that, as you may recall, are strikingly similar to paths in our careers:

- Relational leadership—leadership is horizontal more than vertical. This type of leadership provides for decision-making strategies that allow administrators to hear input from others.
- Leadership for social justice—leadership that intends to change the status quo. This means doing work that changes the lives of students who have not been well served by the status quo in too many of our schools.
- Spiritual leadership—leadership that recognizes spirituality as a source of personal strength as well as a way to understand connectedness to others and to the greater world. Those guided by spiritual leadership are able to move forward to difficult and conflict situations. This style of leadership is guided by passion and hopes, and does not allow it to be silenced. They further note that this style of leadership is particularly evident among women of color.
- Leadership for learning—leadership that holds instruction as the most important part of their work and decisions are made based on student learning as the highest priority.
- Balanced leadership—leadership that strives for balance in home and work (pp. 6–21).

Like us, Grogan and Shakeshaft (2011) determined that these leadership styles are not unique to women; however, they have been sketchily represented in research literature (p. 6). For us, these leadership styles were rarely exhibited in our early educational experiences, and we believe that it is our generation of women and, in particular, women of color who have helped bring these leadership styles into prominence. Valuing these leadership styles can only benefit the children and youth in our P–12 schools.

Lessons for All School Leaders

We are most pleased that our careers, actually our lives, have been dedicated to improving the lives of our students in ways that circumvent and overcome institutional barriers to their learning. In doing so, we have earned our place at the table of school leadership. It has not been easy, and the often-difficult path to respect and equal treatment continues. However, what we know from our experiences and the findings of prominent researchers such as Grogan and Shakeshaft (2011) is that school leadership and the presence of women and people of color are influencing leadership studies in important and substantive ways. We are gratified that men and women from all cultural groups may benefit from our life and career experiences as lessons learned.

It is in the spirit of collaboration with you as a colleague that we review our lessons learned to have you challenge and inform your thinking and that of your school colleagues. We have brought forward the lessons learned from previous chapters for your review. Please read the lessons learned, thoughtfully, and respond to the questions that follow.

Family is important. Family continues to be important. Our immediate families expand to include husbands and their families. Two of our husbands have spent time in the education field, and one is not an educator, and the three spouses are similar in their support for our careers.

Culture is central to how we define ourselves. We recognize the importance of how ethnicity and gender as culture are viewed and experienced by those who have hindered or facilitated our careers. We also recognize the importance of culture in how educators view and regard students in our schools. We find that guiding our educator colleagues to develop the willingness to embrace culture from an assets-based perspective is of innermost importance in our service to our students and their communities.

Multiple mentors are indispensable. Mentoring is crucial to overcome barriers, and it emanates from different directions and sources. Similarly, cross-cultural mentoring, from men and women of other racial and ethnic groups, helped introduce us to the organizational cultures of successful leadership.

Tenacity and perseverance are important to establishing and demonstrating commitment to our vision of what education can be for all students. Without a doubt, our early experiences with discrimination motivated us to seek equitable educational opportunities and outcomes for our students.

- Life brings challenges, and our role as school leaders is to help our colleagues see challenges facing our students and communities.
- Life may not be fair, but we are uniquely positioned to help our students gain the knowledge and skills to have an opportunity to craft their futures.

Change is an intentional process. Personal and systemic change processes are constructed with recognition of the moral imperative of our work. Change processes value the students and communities we serve, are willing to engage those who agree and disagree with equanimity, embrace inequity as important information, and are inclusive and collaborative.

Reflection

In what ways do our lessons learned inform your thinking about your role as an educator? In what ways are these lessons consistent with your values as an educator or educational leader? What barriers currently exist within you or within your school or school district?

_____

_____

_____

_____

What next steps are suggested for you to continue in your development as an educational leader dedicated to serving all students in ways that ensure equitable outcomes?

_____

_____

_____

_____

Your Leadership for Equity Plan

The first step in developing your leadership for equity plan is to summarize your key learning from Chapters 2 through 6. This reflective process will enable you to recognize and understand your value for educational equity, to recognize and build your support systems where appropriate, and to develop a coherent plan for moving forward.

Each chapter afforded one or two opportunities for reflection. Please review your responses and summarize them in the sections provided.

Chapter 2—Your Beginnings

What is it about the early part of your life—where you were born, something about your parents/guardians, opportunities and challenges that you encountered in your community, and recollections of your schooling—that shaped your approach to educating children and youth?

_____

_____

_____

_____

Chapter 3—Your Teacher Years

From your early life, what are some occurrences that have influenced you to become an educator and a leader?

_____

_____

_____

_____

From the early phases of your career, what are some occurrences that have supported your role as a school leader?

_____

_____

_____

_____

Chapter 4—Your Leadership Years

It is not necessary to be an administrator to complete this section. If you are a classroom teacher, school counselor, or other educator practitioner, think of your nonformal role as a school leader.

If you are a veteran educator, what are some experiences that have supported your role as a school leader, whether from the role of teacher, counselor, or administrator? If you are in the first phase of your career as an educator, what are you taking from this section to incorporate into your professional plan?

_____

_____

_____

_____

Reflect on your career thus far—early leadership experiences, mentors who guided your development, and opportunities and challenges that you encountered in the communities you have served.

_____

_____

_____

_____

Chapter 5—Barriers and Cultural Assets

Do you recognize any barriers to your effectiveness across cultural lines? Do you recognize any ways in which you might be unaware of barriers for your students? What might be institutional barriers that exist for students in your school?

_____

_____

_____

_____

In what ways do your core values and those of your school or school district embrace culture? Please use the space provided to describe how a stranger to your school or school district would recognize your commitment to culture as an asset.

_____

_____

_____

_____

Chapter 6—Our Actions

In what ways would a stranger to your school or school district witness behaviors that demonstrate your organization's involvement with closing access and achievement gaps?

_____

_____

_____

_____

Challenges

Take a few moments and review your responses, paying particular attention to personal, professional, and institutional challenges you have faced in providing equitable access and academic outcomes for students. Describe the challenges in this space:

_____

_____

_____

_____

Assets

Now, go back through your responses, this time focusing on your personal assets and your school or school district's assets that support your work for students' equitable access and academic outcomes. Use this space to describe your assets:

_____

_____

_____

_____

Your Actions

Describe one action you will take in the next week that uses your assets to challenge and overcome barriers to students' access and equitable academic outcomes. Please describe the action in this space:

_____

_____

_____

_____

What networks with colleagues are you going to join to support your action?

_____

_____

_____

_____

Please describe what ways you want to improve your craft as an educator?

_____

_____

_____

_____

Envision that it is one year from now. How will you measure your success on this series of actions?

_____

_____

_____

_____

Our Wish for You

Sharing our experiences through the lens of Cultural Proficiency has allowed the three of us to remember the influences that shaped our personal and professional lives. We learned from one another that we share a common passion for changing the conditions for underserved students who rely on us to open the doors of opportunity. This awareness of our shared bond has served to renew our commitments as leaders to do the important work of educational reform. Our professional relationship became a bond of friendship as we learned that we were *sisters of a common cause.*

Through our conversations with one another and with Randy and Stephanie, we also became aware of our differences. This was a powerful reminder to not paint students with a single brush. Learning what makes each student unique is the foundation for meaningful relationships and for creating the bond of trust that is so crucial for students to overcome the impediments to their success. Courage unites us, and commitment to changing the conditions of education inspires us to share our story with you, so that *all children* will succeed. Together with you, our careers contribute to a more open and compassionate future for our students, and their success as learners ensures the future of our nation and world.

Carmella Franco—csfranco1@verizon.net
Maria Ott—Mgott3@aol.com
Darline Robles—drobles5@verizon.net

Resources

Resource A

Carmella S. Franco, EdD

Autobiographical Response to Guiding Questions

Early Life

What are some of the life experiences you have had that facilitated your choice to become an educational leader?

Two major life experiences stand out for me: *My music background or Piano and Boxing.* As both a preschooler and an elementary student, I recall being so impressed by visits to my godparents, great-aunt Susie (I received my middle name Susan from her) and great-uncle Ben's home in Pueblo, Colorado. There I would sit and listen to Uncle Ben play ragtime-style piano on an old upright. The piano was located in their basement, which also housed a boxing gym where kids from the neighborhood hung out. I watched Uncle Ben give them boxing tips, and would also flip through the boxing magazines stacked in a corner of the gym. Little did I know, these two experiences, grounded in my hometown of Pueblo, would have a profound effect in facilitating my rise to becoming an educational leader.

My parents, Al and Margaret, although very young in their parenting role, decided to nurture my interests by buying me an upright piano for my seventh birthday. By this time, we had moved to join my paternal grandparents who had moved from Las Palomas, New

Mexico, to Los Angeles, California. I began my study of piano with teacher Velta Barviks at the Los Angeles Music and Art School (LAMAS), a wonderful community arts facility founded by Pearle Irene Odell.

These lessons would later come into play as I progressed in my career and pursued a doctorate.

1. *Self-discipline and the setting of goals.*

I had to practice the piano each day, in preparation for monthly recitals at the LAMAS. This included weekly memorization assignments. There was no choice—I had to be prepared for a public appearance. I approached all of my responsibilities through this lens of my past studies.

2. *Persistence and determination.*

I learned to never give up. I persisted in my music studies until the material was mastered.

3. *Development of a lifelong hobby.*

As I was seriously working on my study of music, I was, in effect, laying the groundwork for a lifelong love of the arts. Throughout my career, from teacher to superintendent, I have defended the place of the arts in the curriculum. I can speak from personal experience regarding the benefits, and I play for my personal enjoyment to this day.

The interest in boxing had an unusual tie-in with my Saturday music lessons. As a youngster, I recall my father driving me to my lesson while either he sat in to listen or he sat in the car reading the newspaper. From there, we would stop at the Olympic Auditorium and watch the sparring matches. A friend of my father's, Boxer Art Aragon, the Golden Boy (the rights to the name were later sold to Oscar De La Hoya), would chat with him and pat me on the head. To this day, I enjoy watching boxing matches, focusing in on the strategies and techniques of the boxers.

Through my 31 years as a public school administrator and leader, the following lessons from boxing came into play.

- Plan your strategies carefully
- Size up your opponent (person or concept)
- Adjust as the fight unfolds
- Never give up on what you are fighting for
- Get back up and regroup whenever you're knocked down
- Learn from the losses

During my early years in Pueblo, my parents owned and ran a small mom-and-pop grocery store. We lived in the downstairs apartment of my maternal grandparents' home. All of the extended family, meaning grandparents, great-grandparents, great-great-grandparents, great-aunts, and great-uncles, lived within a three-block area. I recall a wonderful time of daily interactions with the family. Pueblo was made up of ethnic neighborhoods. Although Hispanic, we lived in the Italian part of town, and the extended family members spoke fluent Italian. I recall, as a child, entering a room and the language spoken would change from English or Spanish to Italian. My mother's father was fluent in five languages, and my last visit with him prior to his death involved him teaching me basic Italian.

At age five, my mother, father, and younger sister (Christine) boarded a train to Los Angeles. There were two reasons for this permanent move. First, the economy was poor, and second, my father wanted to relocate to be near his parents. My paternal grandparents, who had relocated from near Las Palomas, New Mexico, to California in the mid-1940s, owned three houses on a lot. We moved into the middle house, and settled into a time of new family connections. Two years later, we bought the property from my grandparents, and they moved to another home in El Sereno. One of my fondest memories from the next six years was the Christmas Eve get-together.

My father's five living siblings (two had died in childhood and two as young adults), their spouses, and 21 first cousins would enjoy the holiday spirit. It was a magical time that would not come again, as relatives raised their own families and some moved out of the area or out of state.

Education became an important part of growing up, and I like to think that my immediate family set the stage for this. We moved to Monterey Park, and the expectation was that I would attend college-track classes in high school. All six of us obtained various degrees, with my brother Mitchell and me achieving advanced degrees. I look back with sentimental thoughts, picturing the pride in my Granny's eyes, as I embarked on my career in education. Beyond that, I was fortunate to enjoy the support and encouragement of my parents and that of my husband Tom Jackson throughout my administrative career. The previous experiences provided the backdrop for my choice of educational leader as a goal.

A second life experience involved my active participation in the teacher union. As a new teacher, I found myself in an elementary school that had most of the officers in the district's teacher union. They lost no time getting me involved. I assisted with the writing of the first teacher contract in Rowland Unified School District. I actively participated in a union campaign to elect three board members whose job would be to fire the superintendent. This turned out to a real eye-opener after the three were elected to the board. I spent the next 18 months attending board meetings and watching the superintendent convert the three board members from adversaries to supporters. I wanted to be able to effect change the way he had. I wanted to make a difference on a larger scale. This goal led me to enroll in a program to obtain my administrative services credential. I later earned my doctorate in the area of nontraditional negotiations.

Describe ways you have achieved equitable recognition, visibility, opportunities, identity formation, and balance in your personal and professional life.

I was a college student during the late 1960s and early 1970s, an era of social change. Leadership skills continued to be reinforced during this time. I recall taking philosophy at the end of my freshman year. As the class was under way, I found that the rest of the class participants were juniors and seniors, and I became concerned. However, the worry was for naught. The professor began to put me in charge of groups and projects, and I received the only *A* in the class. I was buoyed and encouraged by this accomplishment, and it clearly set the stage for personal expectations.

Regarding equitable recognition and visibility, I have been fortunate to pursue them at local, state, and national levels. I have always viewed myself as an "organizational" person, meaning I worked hard to further the goals of educational and other types of organizations, and I have served as president of six of these organizations.

It was important that, first, women be accorded the same opportunities as men. Second, it was critical that women of color be viewed as competent leaders, selected on that basis to lead an organization. In four of the organizations to which I achieved this end, the majority of the membership was white.

Even with such a goal, I have never worn a label of identity formation. I view myself first as having been a successful superintendent and educational leader. This included being a role model for employees, for community members, and, most important, for the students. It is to be noted that an all-white board hired me because I met everything they were looking for in a superintendent. That I happened to be Hispanic proved to be the icing on the cake.

It is difficult to strike a balance between the professional and the personal. Many sacrifices have been made during my career, in particular ones involving family. One can certainly attempt to lessen the impact; however, there will be sacrifices. A vivid example of this goes back to the first four months of my superintendency in Whittier City School District. On the night my contract was approved, the board also approved moving forward with a bond. I found myself being out in the community 43 of 46 nights. Is that balance? No—I did what was needed, and luckily, the bond passed. It would have been deadly for me to have my first major challenge as a superintendent fail. I went in running and stayed running—that epitomizes my 12 years in that position.

A Teacher Becoming a Leader

Describe the day you decided you wanted to become a school leader.

The day I decided to become a school leader stands out vividly in my mind. I determined that I wanted to become a teacher when I was in seventh grade. This was because I really enjoyed school and my teachers called on me often to tutor fellow classmates who were struggling with their reading or math.

I had such positive experiences with my elementary school teachers that it was inevitable that I would decide to become a teacher. The years of serving as a "teacher's helper" and classroom tutor for those who needed extra assistance paved the way for me.

The teachers invariably called on girls to serve in classroom leadership roles. I was always selected to lead projects, from overseeing the construction of a castle and moat (studying the Middle Ages) to correcting papers of spelling and math tests. As part of the project phase, I had to select other students who I thought could successfully work as a team. This was a challenge, as everyone wanted to be called on to participate. In retrospect, this leadership role provided training for personnel selection later on in my career. My classmates called me "the professor," a nickname that helped nudge me along the route to becoming a teacher. My gender definitely enhanced my access to leadership roles. I do not recall any boys ever being given this opportunity during my elementary school years. I was an English-only speaker, one of a few in my school setting. My proficiency in English, both spoken and written, probably placed me at an advantage in a school that was at least 95% Hispanic. I did not feel at a disadvantage not knowing Spanish, as none of the teachers knew it either. However, my ear was tuned to it; I wanted to learn the language; and I ultimately learned it, beginning in fifth grade. I carried a Spanish/English dictionary with me everywhere I went. My paternal grandmother, Teresa Torres Padilla, played an important role in assisting me with this goal. It took some convincing on my part, as she spoke only English to her more than 20 grandchildren. From college until her passing, we spoke nearly daily—in Spanish! From first grade on, each of my elementary school teachers encouraged me to succeed. By all accounts, I was an overachiever, eager to please, and I was told that I would go far in life.

My decision to become a school leader, however, took place in other circumstances. As a music major in college, I was studying with Dr. Milton Stern at California State University, Los Angeles (CSULA). It was my second year—I was 19 years old. Sometime during the lesson, Dr. Stern asked me about my career goals. I answered that I wanted to become a school principal. This decision preceded becoming a public school teacher. In essence, I already knew that I wanted to lead. From the solitary experience with my piano, I wanted to expand to lead others. In a reflective sense, the inner strength developed, waiting to be of use.

My first job interview took place with a very strict and business-like principal. I was to become part of a third-grade team of teachers, working with gifted and talented students in an open classroom setting. It was one of the most challenging and exciting assignments of my life, that is, keeping up with eight-year-old students who were reading at 9th–12th-grade level. What a unique and marvelous experience this proved to be!

I encountered major barriers because of gender. In my second year of teaching, I made an appointment with human resources (personnel, in those days), and when I stated that I had the goal of becoming a principal, I was told, "Why would a nice, young woman like you want to be a principal?" Still, I requested that I be considered at some future time. That same month, I went to CSULA to investigate entering the administrative credential master's degree program. An appointment had been set with the dean of the department, which was all male. Again, I was told that I was only 23 years old. I was told to obtain an MA in another curricular area and then come back. I knew I had the gift of time, so I did just that. I obtained an MA in elementary education, focused some of my research on women in administration, and then returned to pursue my administrative credential. The number of women in the classes had increased to about 20%. The second time around, I encountered no objections from the dean.

The Rowland Unified School District assignment was a godsend. I had had four other offers and thank the day I joined the district. The curriculum and instruction professional development that the district conducted prepared me for my first administrative position as a specialist, and subsequently, my first principalship.

After four years in central office, I was ready for a principalship. However, none was available, given the "35 years or older" rule of thumb for the hiring of principals.

More than 100 applicants were interested in two principalships open in the neighboring Bassett Unified School District, and I was one of the two selected. I recall being asked in a final interview, "By the way, how old are you?" I took a deep breath and responded, "30 years old; but I am sure that will have no bearing on my selection for the position." School law, especially related to personnel, had become a pet interest of mine, and I was well aware of the legalities involved with hiring practices.

Administrative Roles

As a teacher, I was thrown into leadership roles beginning my second year. That year, the teacher union asked me to be on the team that wrote the first teacher contract for Rowland Unified School District. I spent countless nights at the local California Teachers' Association (CTA) offices being trained on how to construct the contract. In another occurrence, my peers at the site elected me one of their representatives to the School Advisory Committee (SAC). This experience enhanced my interactions with parents, colleagues, and district office staff. Additionally, my principal placed me in charge of multicultural activities (Cinco de Mayo) and other performances for parents. This increased my exposure in the district and in the local school community.

My visibility and expertise caught the eye of the new assistant superintendent of instruction, and I was ultimately selected for a position in the reorganized division. It was an ideal time, with instruction the number one focus. The development of the new cadre of specialists became a work in progress. I benefited greatly by gaining experience in a multitude of areas: intermediate level science adoption; high school course revision process; nurses' handbook revision; assisting with staff development activities for teachers, principals, and other administrators. When I moved on to my first principalship four years later, I felt extremely well prepared.

I entered an administrative credential program at age 25, and completed it two years later. I obtained my first administrative position as a bilingual/English as Second Language (ESL) specialist at age 27. Some of the personal qualities that helped me with that entry position included the following.

- Knowledge about the area of specialty (e.g., I taught in the district's first Title VII bilingual program for four years.)
- A sense of political awareness (e.g., I made a point of introducing myself to principals and senior managers so they knew who I was. I had also met several board members.)
- Persistence in the pursuit of my career goals (e.g., I mapped paths for achieving my career goals.)
- Support from a mentor

Assistant Superintendent Dr. Dolores Smith became a mentor at work. She signed me up for my first Association of California School Administrators (ACSA) Committee, and made sure that I joined the Women in Educational Leadership (WEL) organization based in Los Angeles. That also started my lifelong involvement in organizations, which would prove extremely important and fulfilling as I moved through leadership roles.

I observed from the start that I would need to prove myself doubly in every administrative position. I made sure that I had all the credentials; I attended workshop after workshop designed for women who wanted to succeed and, in effect, break through the glass ceiling; I observed those female leaders who had made it to the ranks of senior management. None were Hispanic, so I had no role models in that regard other than some in the Los Angeles Unified School District (LAUSD) system who were involved with WEL.

Having the opportunity to serve the students and community of a heavily Latino district was a joy because their success in the educational process would be my daily work. Test scores soared during my four years as principal of a K–5 school, and the same scenario took place as I went on to serve at the feeder middle school. I had the children of most of the board members at the K–5 level, and they wanted me to follow their children on to the Grades 6–8 experience. The middle school teachers and I forged a strong partnership to have students succeed, and the fruits of those efforts were many. Every eighth grader left with a full study of three careers, and they knew the educational preparation that was needed. To this day, most of my department chairs from that special time still get together at my home at least once a year. I was richer and blessed to have had their support in erasing the barriers to student success. It was both humbling and rewarding to see parents looking ahead to future college and university studies for their children.

While curriculum and instruction were my first love, personnel took a close second. That is the crossroads I came to, as I had to decide about my next career step. A doctoral classmate, who also was a principal in the district, recruited me to the Lennox School District. In my final interview, I was told that I would be well prepared for the superintendency if I accepted the personnel director position. In Lennox, the district was known as a major port of entry for Latino immigrants from Mexico and Central/South America. It was wonderful to be able to hire cream-of-the-crop teachers who would influence students on a daily basis. This setting provided many opportunities to further develop my leadership skills.

My six years in Lennox included the highlights of working with three schools to achieve California Distinguished School status and of cowriting with professors from California State University, Dominguez Hills, the largest new teacher-training grant in California. Students in a more than 95% Latino school district realized tremendous successes—there was indeed no limit to what they could achieve. This mission drove my desire to lead my school district. Thus, when Whittier City beckoned, I answered.

One of my mentors, via the University of La Verne (ULV) doctoral program, was Dr. Patricia Clark White, who was a superintendent in Orange County, California. She served as a member of my dissertation committee, and was the first person I called when I obtained my superintendent position.

Obtaining my doctorate was a highlight of my professional career. Once I made up my mind to pursue this advanced degree, I religiously put on blinders, and allowed no distractions in my quest to reach this acme of professional growth. I completed the program in three years, placing in the top 5% of my class. Achieving that end, I then wrote the dissertation in eight months, focusing on the topic of nontraditional negotiations. Besides the professional growth, I gained much in the personal reflection that this exceptional doctoral program encouraged. I also felt a great deal of support from the dean and professors in the program. It truly was a unique time in my life.

During my K–5 principalship, I learned many lessons. I continued to expand my political awareness, and this was made easy because I had the children/grandchildren of all five board members. It was common to have daily visits from board members, which I duly reported on back to my superintendent at the time. At the site, I had four teachers who had been principals in the school district. I was a 31-year-old principal, and the staff members were 15 years and older than I. This would have been enough of a challenge without the four former principals. I turned the table on this one, and I began to seek their advice and expertise in certain areas. They gave me their 100% support, and helped me to be even more successful in my four years at that site. The staff also wanted me to communicate with them in different ways. It was my style to go out and track down a teacher or aide, and discuss an item. I learned to accommodate those who preferred a written communication.

When the board members' fifth-grade children went on to the middle school, the board asked the interim superintendent if I could also move to the sixth–eighth-grade school. And off I went!

The Superintendency

I was recruited and selected as superintendent of the Whittier City School District in the 24th year of my educational career. It was an exciting and heady time for me. I was one of five finalists, four men, one of whom was a sitting superintendent, and I was the only woman and the only ethnic minority. The community was 85% Hispanic at the time, and I was later informed by a board member that me being Hispanic and bilingual was the icing on the cake. I was further informed that I met everything they were looking for in a new superintendent. My 12 years as superintendent, prior to retirement, were extremely meaningful in practices and programs implemented and, also, from the self-learning process that went hand-in-hand with the job.

The State Trusteeship

In March of 2010, I received a call from ACSA, the California state administrator organization, asking if I was amenable to having my name submitted for a state trustee position for academic failure of a school district. I responded that it sounded like an interesting position. I was told I would hear something about the process in the near future. I received a call from the California State Department of Education asking for my resume. At the end of April, the process went into full swing. I had a series of telephone interviews over a two-day period, and I was then asked to fly to Sacramento for additional interviews. Following the interviews, it became clear that my name would be considered for an appointment at the State Board of Education (SBE) meeting (May 5, 2010).

During the meeting, the SBE discussed which option to assign to the Alisal trusteeship. I was assigned Option B (California Education Code Section 52055.57(c)(3)), which entailed having ultimate authority, that is, all authority was stripped from the Alisal board, as were their stipends and health benefits. It was a first in the state. There had been major board upheaval and a fracturing of the board/superintendent relationship, which was polarizing the staff and community. The students' educations were negatively impacted. Student performance was already in shambles, with 10 of the 11 schools, including the district, in program-improvement status. My appointment was for academic failure of the district and its students, fueled by adult problems.

I am encountering daily challenges, and I am focusing primarily on bringing stability to the governance, leadership, and instructional areas of the district.

What do you feel are some of your really strong qualities as a leader? What do you feel is your strong personal quality that helped you in your leadership position?

- *Persistence.* As noted earlier, when dissuaded from entering the administrative credential program, I made a brief detour, and then successfully returned to my goal. I put on blinders when I began work on my doctorate. I completed the required three years of coursework, and wound up in the top 5% of the class. It's recommended that doctoral candidates take 18 to 24 months to complete the dissertation. I wrote mine in eight months, something I do not recommend to others. It was good to have it completed, however.

My husband, family, and friends were especially supportive of my goals. During the doctoral work, I became acutely aware of something: I could count the number of Hispanics on one hand, and that was out of nearly 200 in the cohort. It was a self-mandate to excel and represent my ethnic and cultural group well. Beyond that, I was self-motivated and self-driven, and the drive to succeed was heavily intrinsic.

- *Competence.* It was important that all credentials were obtained, including the doctorate. There should be no question regarding my competence in the field. The administrative paths that I pursued enhanced my preparation as a principal, a director, and, ultimately, a superintendent.

- *Demand the best.* I demanded the best from and had high expectations of both others and myself. For example, the image of the school district was a major responsibility. I was known for editing, and the dreaded "red pen." This included, in particular, presentations to the board. I often perused budget presentations, finding items that needed editing or correction. As time passed, in my superintendency, I finally gave myself some latitude to err.

- *Hard worker.* This is best exemplified by the General Obligation Bond and Mello-Roos Bond, which entailed me being out in the community nearly every night and on weekends. My visibility in Whittier helped contribute to a more positive view of the school district, which facilitated the passage of two bond issues.

- *Visionary.* One thing near and dear to my heart was the importance of libraries in the schools. In partnership with the Rose Hills Foundation and the hard work of the principals, between 2001 and 2008, when I retired, each of the elementary schools enjoyed a brand new library.

  I wanted the school district to provide every opportunity for students to have above and beyond the "normal" school experience. Overseeing the securing of 12 million dollars in outside funds (e.g., grants) helped to accomplish this end.

- *Excellent communicator.* The development of strategies to relay the school district's message was critical. This included oral and written communications (e.g., polished newsletters) along with personal interactions.

- *Collaborator and bridge builder.* Working closely with government agencies, both state and city, and employee groups over the years contributed to a successful tenure as superintendent. This was carried out further when I was selected interim superintendent of the Woodland Joint Unified School District. While there was not always agreement, there was certainly a respect for differing opinions and a genuine effort on my part for all to work together in a collaborative fashion in the best interest of students.

- *Ability to work well with boards of education.* With a few exceptions, and only where board member egos interfered, the relationship between the superintendent and the board was one where I worked tirelessly. There was frequent turnover at election time in Whittier, and it was incumbent on me to know the board members and build relationships. I am grateful to the board that hired me and, after that, to several who were particularly supportive of my efforts to serve the students and their families. During my interim superintendency in Woodland, I enjoyed building relationships with the seven-member board. It proved to be an eventful, challenging, and magical year, and I am thankful for the opportunity the board provided to me.

  If I had to cite a facet of my style that contributed to good board/superintendent relations, it would be equitable and fair treatment of the individual members, whether I agreed with them. Additionally, relationships were kept professional, no matter who came on and off the board.

- *See both sides of issues.* The ability to stand back, cross over the fence, and stand in the other person or organization's shoes is one of my greatest strengths. It contributed to a sense of empathy and understanding. I spent much time on this with my senior managers, helping them to see the benefits of doing so.

- *Make hard decisions.* I have always said that I was not in my position to win a popularity contest. Feathers were ruffled and feelings were hurt, no doubt, in the quest to achieve excellence and meet students' educational needs. We all want to be liked; however, many superintendents sacrifice their integrity in the process. I was not willing to do that when difficult decisions had to be made. From the closing of schools (two in Whittier and two in Woodland) to unpopular budget reductions, the best interest of students and the district guided my decision recommendations.

- *Political astuteness.* Superintendents who cannot deal with the politics of the job would be well served to consider a career move. Superintendency has been cited as being one of the most political jobs around. Every decision made appears to have some political ramification or consequence in today's world. I like politics, and navigated the shark-ridden waters of the job on a daily basis. Whenever an issue arose (e.g., more than 100-foot poles for a wireless system), the array of consequences would flash before my eyes. That one almost caused me to stop breathing. Then time would be devoted to exploring the pros and cons and developing strategies to offset the negatives if that were the desired direction.

What do you feel are some of the important qualities for women (women of color) leaders in education?

- Competence
- Outstanding oral and written skills
- Ability to relate to *all* races, ethnicities, social and economic classes, and, in particular, the Anglo establishment

Please describe some of the difficulties you have experienced as a woman of color administrator.

- *Had to work twice as hard.* I noticed over time that I was appearing at numerous events, whereas other colleagues would make occasional appearances. I had to go above and beyond in bringing positive recognition to my school district. I believe that working twice as hard and being in a constant pursuit of excellence characterizes my entire career.
- *Experienced professional jealousy.* When asked to assume a key leadership role in a professional organization, I encountered remarks that can be construed to be of a jealous nature. No overt action was taken; however, it was readily obvious that another individual wanted my position.
- *Encountered unsupportive (female and male) supervisors.* In several instances, attempts were made by a supervisor to discourage my seeking other promotional opportunities. My time frame for advancement was delayed; however, persistence on my

part and assistance from other mentors ameliorated this situation. Ultimately, I was successful, but I would have experienced more rapid advancement had there not been this level of obstruction.

- *Increases in the number of women in administration have been threatening in and of itself; adding color to it is an additional complexity.* I am aware of cases where women of color have been hired into administrative positions where there was definite resentment by white males in the organization. Some women survived it, and some did not. Some, I believe, were purposely set up to fail. I personally encountered the resentment situation, and, unlike a number of the cases observed, it did not result in a failure on my part. These examples highlight the particular importance for women of color to carefully assess the districts and positions for which they are applying. No good ever came out of being set up for failure, and, if one looks closely, the clues are there.

- *Saw, in the end, that it has been an asset for me.* The difficulties and challenges I faced definitely made me a stronger person, honed my survival skills, and gave me insights in to the political machinations for working in the educational administrative arena. In today's climate, it is not for the faint of heart. The challenge is not only to survive but to succeed.

How do women become identified with being in charge, without being identified with negative or unfeminine ways?

This is an interesting point. Obviously, women need to learn to play with the "big boys," but I don't interpret this as acting like them. That being said, I believe that both men and women in leadership roles portray themselves in distinct ways:

- Conducting business in a conservative and serious manner
- Being viewed as a business leader, in charge of a million-dollar operation
- Dressing appropriately for the position (e.g., business attire, dark suits)

I enjoyed wearing scarves, and they became a signature item for me over the years. I never wore nail polish; however, many other women leaders did. Personally, I saw it as a distraction to how I wanted to be perceived. My stance was a no-nonsense approach.

The issue of negative perceptions of women being in charge will be there as long as there is a dearth of women in top CEO positions. This has been a hard wheel to turn, and it continues to move very slowly. The logical interpretation is that women are not viewed as being able to run a major business; consequently, men continue to be named to those positions. When a woman does break through a glass ceiling, extreme scrutiny follows. Her every move and word comes under the microscope. I recall observing some of the male leaders, as I moved through the administrative chairs, and they were tough negotiators. The female role models, while nurturing, were tough also. In retrospect, while I might have come across a bit hard lined, that was counter to whom I really was. Lessons learned: To the point of femininity, I have learned that being a strong leader did not mean I had to be unfriendly, and being warm and approachable did not need to signify weakness. Those lessons did not come easily, and it would have been good if a mentor had shared that with me early in my administrative career.

In what ways are the issues surrounding authority similar for a male and female leader, specifically women of color?

The professional failures of women of color in the past two decades, in particular, colored (pardon the pun) how we were and are viewed. I recall being told if a Latina had failed in a superintendent role in a school district that I was interested in, that would not be the best place for me to go because of perceptions. I would ask, "Why should that be the case?" More recently, that conversation has involved both men and women of color in the same breath.

Superintendents are hired by boards of education, a group of individuals with their own backgrounds of views, opinions, and prejudices. There are boards that collectively and individually do not have confidence in a woman of color. Some have heard something negative about a former superintendent of color from a nearby school district. In some cases, the most damning are arrogant male board members, white and those of color, who have problems taking recommendations from a female superintendent of color. Their upbringing does not allow women to rise to a position of authority. Unfortunately, boards with this mentality are not a match for an aspiring woman leader of color.

The lesson learned here is to do one's homework regarding the board members. A heartening note is that the previously mentioned description does not represent all board members, male or female. A great deal of education on this topic needs to be conducted with all board members, but in particular, with those in minority affiliations. One important way to overcome this barrier is the growth of our reputations as successful educational leaders, who just happen to be of color.

Please describe some of the differences you have observed in the ways men and women work.

- There are men who cannot relate to women *and* women who cannot relate to women.
- Men do business on the golf course; women at lunch and dinner (e.g., sports issue).
- Women are much more detail oriented.
- Women are sometimes more aware of nuances.

Please describe ways you have struggled for equitable recognition, visibility opportunities, identity formation, and balance in your personal and professional life.

- Equitable recognition and visibility opportunities: I actively pursued these at local, state, and national levels.
- I have not personally experienced problems with movement into organizational leadership positions. Women of color need to be involved in organizations, especially those with high numbers of Anglo memberships.
- Identity formation: I have never worn a label.
- I view myself as having been a successful superintendent and educator.
- I am a role model for employees, community members, and my students.
- The all-white board that hired me viewed having a Hispanic at the helm of the district as a positive asset.

What do you feel are some of the important personal qualities, values, and behaviors necessary for the following?

Leadership and instructional improvement

- Strong communication skills
- Trust building
- High expectations
- No excuses
- Lots of support
- Strong staff development
- Pursuit of excellence in everything attempted

Teacher evaluation and support

- Identify weak links.
- Provide support/opportunity for improvement.
- If no improvement, help them move on.
- Provide staff with professional development.
- Allow staff leeway and creativity to develop quality staff development programs.

Community/school board relations

- Keep them informed! I sent out extensive updates, most in a newsletter format.

Relations with students and families

- They are Number 1.
- Respond to all parent calls and correspondence.
- Send notes to parents and students.

Story of Nellie and David

The school where I served my first principalship was in deplorable physical condition. During the first month, I sent out a flyer asking for volunteer assistance from any parents connected with landscaping. One morning, as I was out in front of the school greeting students and parents, a van pulled up and David and Nellie Castro offered their assistance. They wound up installing sprinklers in the front planter, which ran the length of the building, and planting rose-bushes. I still keep in touch with this warm and generous couple, and I am most grateful for what they did to improve the school environment for students and the community.

What do you feel are some of the important personal qualities, values, and behaviors necessary for leadership and instructional improvement?

Strong communication skills. I was very lucky to have developed strong written communication skills at an early age. Those have served me well throughout my career. I have had to work a bit harder on the oral communication area. Only in recent years have I have felt comfortable speaking to large groups. Probably some of that ease has come with the frequent speaking engagements that I have had in my last two roles: interim superintendent and state trustee.

Trust building. A leader needs to be able to generate trust to enlist followers in the vision, mission, and dream for an organization. The way that I have carried out this behavior is through actions matching my words. I wanted to be known as a person who keeps her word.

High expectations. I have always refused to settle for less than the highest expectations, especially as it applied to what we were doing for students and their families. When parents heard that I was going to see that their children had experiences and programs like those in higher-economic settings (e.g., Beverly Hills), they were ecstatic. It generated a tremendous amount of parental support for the schools.

No excuses. No excuses are acceptable in my estimation. I believe that education should *radiate possibilities*. The question should always be, What can I do to improve things?

Lots of support. With the field of education, including the teaching profession, as challenging as it is today, it is so important for leaders to provide the necessary support. This can include moral support in addition to support that includes assistance, materials, and professional development to name a few. Sometimes, just a note of encouragement is all that is needed to keep a new or a veteran teacher going.

Please describe some of the approaches you use in problem solving and decision making.

- Thorough analysis with a variety of options
- Involvement of different groups (e.g., administrators, teachers, classified staff, and parents)
- Informational meetings and written communication

What are the most satisfying accomplishments and rewards of your educational leadership career?

- Established the vision as superintendent for a school district
- Oversaw improvements in student achievement
- Hired top-notch administrators, teachers, confidential, and classified staff
- Negotiated successful multiyear contracts with the bargaining units
- Brought all salaries to a highly competitive level in comparison to the prior level
- Experienced strong support from the community (e.g., passed two bonds in three and a half years)
- Enacted major changes (e.g., boundaries with a minimum of upheaval)
- Returned district to neighborhood-school status
- President of six organizations

What would you advise to those who are considering roles in educational leadership?

- Take the responsibility of representing children seriously.
- Don't forget your roots.
- Set your goals and accomplish them.
- Do what you do *well*.
- Blaze the trail for those who will follow.

Reflective Thoughts

As I reflect on my life's journey, it is clear that my identity as a female, as a Latina leader, and as a role model for both children and adults has been a strength. I have used the professional and personal experiences; I have aligned those experiences like the pieces of a mosaic, and I have served to nurture and encourage those who needed it most. Challenges and adversities that I have encountered have been measured against the greater good, spurring me on to ensure that all students can learn and be successful. In this new phase of the journey, I return to the lessons of my early days of studying piano. That is, I will never give up in my quest as a leader to see that children receive the high-quality education that they deserve.

Resource B

Maria G. Ott, PhD

Response to Guiding Questions

What are some of the life experiences you have had that facilitated your choice to become an educational leader?

On a personal level, I believe that my journey to learn English and succeed as a student both at the elementary and secondary levels built deep compassion for students who are taking the same journey to succeed academically. It is interesting when I hear others describe their kindergarten and first-grade experiences, and all I have is darkness. The darkness reflects the fear and anxiety that accompanied my introduction to school, a new culture, and a new, extended family.

When my mother, brother, and I arrived from Germany, I was five years old, and we moved in with my father's sister and her family in East Los Angeles. The house was too small to accommodate all of us comfortably, but my father's family made the best of the difficult arrangement. Eventually, my father was able to rent a small house near his sister. I started kindergarten at Gravois Avenue Elementary School, moving on to Sacred Heart Catholic School. The only memories that remain from those early days in school are recollections of uncomfortable situations. I still remember coming home with a worksheet that had my last name misspelled, and I repeated to my mother how my teacher said my name was pronounced. My mother was upset that the teacher did not get my name right. When she told me that the teacher was wrong, I cried. "How could my teacher be wrong?" I thought.

In elementary school, I acquired tenacity about doing well in school, and I would stay up late, trying to get my schoolwork right. I remember my parents talking to my teachers about my habit of erasing my work until it was right. That is why many of my papers ended up with holes from erasures. My mother had the job of trying to help with my homework, which was frustrating for both of us since my mother's education from Germany was different in content and method from what was expected in my classes. It was only after having my children that I learned how important the homework experience is for children. My parents were incredibly supportive in that they insisted that I do my best in school, wanting more for me than was available in their school years. The fact that homework is a cultural experience for mainstream American students should not be overlooked when thinking about ways to help English learners and children who are socioeconomically disadvantaged.

Finally, a student in my husband's eighth-grade classroom convinced me that I could make a difference for students. Tutoring this Hispanic-immigrant student connected me with the fulfillment of unlocking knowledge for a young person and convinced me that teaching was my calling.

Describe ways you have achieved equitable recognition, visibility, opportunities, identity formation, and balance in your personal and professional life.

After two years of teaching special education, I accepted the opportunity to teach in one of the Title VII-funded bilingual programs in the Los Angeles Unified School District. This opportunity was especially gratifying since it demonstrated that I was correct about the potential of the students in my special education class. Although they were described as mentally retarded, they appeared to me to be there because they were Hispanic and had not mastered academic English. At that time in my career, I did not have the research knowledge about why academic English was essential to learning. I naturally knew what was needed for success because I had walked in those English-learner shoes, and I understood that mastery of academic knowledge was essential for student success. Moving from special education to bilingual education was an opportunity to impact more students and prevent their placement in a restrictive environment.

The Title VII bilingual program was considered a model for attaining literacy in two languages. Educators visited from throughout the nation to observe our work as teachers. At first, I was nervous about having so many observers during my Spanish instruction; however, the experience built my confidence as a teacher leader. My principal asked me to become a master teacher for student teachers from California State University at Los Angeles, and I was assigned a teacher to guide and supervise each semester. This was particularly gratifying because I learned to be a reflective educator during the daily discussions with my student teachers related to my practice.

The team of Title VII teachers received intensive and ongoing training to develop our expertise in delivery of content instruction in two languages. At the time, I did not realize that my training was unique and that the investment in my learning would lay the foundation for my career growth and eventual selection to serve as a school district superintendent. My experiences in the bilingual program led to my selection as teacher and coordinator for the English as a Second Language program at an elementary school in the El Sereno area of East Los Angeles. This experience opened the door to further administrative experiences.

I was asked to join the team of instructional specialists assigned to the region of LAUSD that encompassed the eastside of the district, and it was my role to provide classroom demonstrations, develop curriculum, design professional development experiences, and assist the team in responding to school-level requests for instructional assistance. In this role, the regional superintendent came to know my work, and when a vice principal position opened at Murchison Street School, I received a special appointment because of my bilingual skills. This appointment was an acknowledgment by the superintendent that I had demonstrated the potential to succeed as an administrator.

After three and one-half years as a vice principal, I took the promotional exam for principal and placed in the top 5% on the eligibility list. It was during this time that I realized how challenging it was to maintain a career and raise a family. My two children were still in grade school, and I found it increasingly more difficult to balance the demands of my career and the needs of my children and husband. My husband started law school while I was working as a coordinator and instructional specialist. It was necessary for my husband to spend long hours attending classes and, later, studying for the bar exam. When aspiring administrators ask about how I balanced my career and my personal life, I admit that it was not easy. Without the support of my family, I would have missed opportunities for career success because the choices were limited—meet career expectations or give up advancement opportunities.

My mother provided child care for my children during their early years, and when I was appointed principal, I hired a child care provider to come into my home. My children were active in sports and activities, including scouting. In retrospect, I think my husband and I managed to keep balance during the stresses of pursuing our individual careers. My husband developed a career as an attorney and eventually a CEO while I became a principal, a central office administrator, and finally, a superintendent.

One of the challenges I faced in advancing my career as a leader for all children occurred while I was a central office administrator. I became well known for my leadership in the area of bilingual education, and I had several opportunities to appear on national television to discuss effective approaches for English learners. My first opportunity at the central office involved leading the Eastman curriculum design program. I benefited from the foundations established by my predecessor Bonnie Rubio, who was principal of Eastman Avenue Elementary School during the time that the California Department of Education was attempting to implement curriculum design models built on the theoretical framework that included research related to the acquisition of academic English. As the leader of the Eastman curriculum design project, I worked with 28 schools committed to implementing a structured approach to a bilingual education.

I was promoted to a larger leadership role in the central office of instruction, but everyone viewed me as the bilingual program expert. When I sought to move into a mainstream leadership position, I continued to find that others viewed me through the narrower lens of bilingual programs. In one conversation with a superintendent from another district who was looking for an assistant superintendent, I was asked if I would consider taking the role of categorical programs director. Now, when I mentor administrators, I encourage them to seek broad experiences and avoid the narrowing of their potential by leaders who might only see them as an individual who can solve a district's categorical issues.

Describe the day you decided you wanted to become a school leader.

I clearly remember the day I decided that I wanted to become a school leader. I had been teaching second grade as a bilingual teacher. I was determined that no student would leave my class without reading well and, at minimum, at grade level. The school used a divided-day approach to reading instruction so that half the class attended in the morning and the other half in the afternoon. It seemed like such a missed opportunity to send half the students home, so I requested that my class remain for the full day without a split for reading. In this way, I was able to give all students extra support. I pushed the students every minute of the day to get maximum growth. One day, I was listening to a third-grade teacher talk about her program. She had received several of my students, and she described what I considered a mediocre experience for these students. I remember thinking that I had worked so hard to advance my students, and now they were getting only an adequate learning opportunity. It struck me that the principal of the school was crucial in monitoring what teachers do during the school day. This realization made me want to have an impact on a whole school.

The principalship still seemed far removed from my career goals, but I couldn't help think that if I ever had the opportunity, I would want all teachers to work together to raise the expectation bar. I knew that as someone who had overcome the impediments of being socio-economically disadvantaged, it took teachers who pushed me to high levels. I wanted this for all children.

In what ways did your gender enhance or limit access to your early leadership roles?

Gender surfaced during my first assignment as principal. I was the first woman assigned to Hart Street School in Canoga Park, most of the administrators in the area were male, and they were fond of reminding me and the other new female administrators that we were not part of the club. The comments did not bother me because I felt that my appointment as principal was evidence that I was on an equal footing with my male counterparts. Sometimes comments were made that would be considered sexist now; however, at that time, males behaved in ways that were offensive but accepted in the workplace. I remember being introduced as someone who was "good looking." Good looking had nothing to do with my success in the exam process for principal, so I just disregarded the remarks. Later, when I was selected as the superintendent for the Little Lake City School District, the headline in the local newspaper read "Latina Appointed." I was the first woman to lead the district, and I was also the first person of color. On a personal level, being the "first woman" was reflection of my hard work and talent, and I did not feel the impediments that many women of my era described. The reason that being a woman limited access was more at the personal level because I was trying to have it all—a successful career and a successful personal life. This was the hardest part of being a woman in a leadership role.

When I read the research about women who attend single-gender schools, I learned that my years at a coinstitutional high school where all the girls attended separate classrooms from the boys prepared me to be successful. The fact that I attended a college for women also prepared me to succeed in a profession dominated by male leadership. I was educated to believe in myself and to tackle any challenge to make a difference that would matter to society. Attending Mount Saint Mary's College was truly an experience that would alter my career potential. Not only was I the first in my family to attend college but also I benefited from an education designed to help women succeed in life and in their careers.

How did your culture enhance or limit access to your early leadership roles?

The greatest obstacle that I faced in relationship to my culture was overcoming expectations. As the oldest child in the Gutierrez family, I had no role models that were available to guide me as I prepared to graduate from a Catholic high school. My teachers helped me shape dreams of a better life. My parents were hardworking, saving to pay for Catholic schooling at the elementary and secondary level. As an adult, I have come to appreciate the sacrifices made by my parents. My father worked as a barber, and he worked six days a week to make a living. My mother was frugal, and saved by making all the clothes for the family and preparing economical meals. The humble beginnings of both my parents, and our humble lifestyle, produced four successful adults, three of the four graduated from college. I earned a PhD, and I continue to attribute my success to the hard work that characterized every aspect of my upbringing. My father's family came to the United States during the Mexican Revolution in search of work and a better life for their children. The Gutierrez family was large, and they valued their time together. Typically, the family gathered for picnics in the park to celebrate special events—birthdays, holidays, and bridal and baby showers. I remember feeling most accepted for who I was when I was with my cousins. There were no pretenses, and we were proud to be Mexican Americans.

Since culture defines us, I believe that my early leadership roles were positively influenced by the work ethic, appreciation for being

Mexican American, and the respect for my first culture (German) that were demonstrated in my family. We struggled economically, yet we were rich in life experiences.

Describe the role of mentors at this stage of your career.

My first mentors were white males who encouraged me to take on significant leadership roles. In retrospect, I believe that I benefited from opportunities that were provided because of my ability to work collaboratively, to demonstrate instructional knowledge, and to be a passionate advocate for children living in poverty. I challenged my colleagues and my supervisors to find ways to help children who were struggling because of language-learning issues, and I was not afraid to challenge the status quo regarding student achievement issues.

My early mentors opened doors of advancement that would have been impossible to open on my own. When I became a coordinator at the school level, it was because of males who recognized leadership potential that I did not have the experiences to realize on my own. If someone had asked me about my aspirations, I would have said it was my goal to help failing children overcome barriers present in our public schools. Yet my white, male supervisors would have said that I had the potential to climb in the leadership ranks. I found it startling to think that others had higher aspirations than those that I saw in my future.

When I read the stories of other Latinas that had achieved high levels of success, I realized that we were a club of women who had benefited from the open-minded viewpoints of white, male supervisors who were willing to extend a hand to help us climb beyond the glass ceiling.

Later in my career, I was blessed to find outstanding Latinas who served as my mentors and guided me to realize that I could become a superintendent. My first significant mentor was Amelia McKenna, who was an associate superintendent in LAUSD. Amelia McKenna demonstrated her expertise in multiple leadership roles, and she was acknowledged across the school district as a leader to be respected and admired. She selected me as an administrator in her division, which was responsible for all language acquisition issues in the LAUSD. I remember working with Amelia McKenna as one of the most rewarding experiences of my career. Ms. McKenna had a brave heart for children learning English as a second language and for children of poverty. Like me, Amelia McKenna was a Latina with interesting cultural roots, descending from a Scotsman who worked building the railroad in Mexico. Amelia McKenna trusted my judgment, and we became an inseparable team for the children in LAUSD who needed advocates at the top of the LAUSD organization.

My second significant mentor was Darline Robles, who was an assistant superintendent in the Montebello Unified School District when I met her in the USC doctoral program. We became great colleagues and friends. It was Dr. Robles who encouraged me to apply for the superintendent's position in the Little Lake City School District. This position seemed out of reach and out of context for a career spent in the LAUSD. Yet Darline Robles counseled and encouraged me. She saw potential that was not visible to me, and I took the leap. When I was selected as the superintendent of Little Lake, I celebrated with Amelia McKenna and Darline Robles and thanked them for their support and counsel.

What do you see as your strong personal qualities that helped you in your initial leadership position?

Tenacity is a quality that I acquired early in my life. Coming to a new country as a five-year-old child, learning about my father's family and his culture, learning English and later Spanish, and overcoming stereotypes about Mexican Americans during the 1960s and 1970s instilled in me a deep determination to not give in to those who saw me as someone limited by my background. I developed a strong backbone when it came to staying the course related to my obligations. I succeeded in college and achieved graduate degrees at the master's and doctoral levels. When I look at my resume, I see that I stayed in positions long enough to leave an impact. It would have been easy to move early in my career, and I was even offered a promotional opportunity that I did not accept to fulfill my personal need to make a difference at the principal level.

Because I experienced prejudice and intolerance as a young adult, I acquired a deep and unwavering sense of compassion and commitment to children who were learning English and who were striving to be the first in their families to graduate from high school and go on to college. I always share my personal story of struggle and success with families in my community so that I will be a role model that inspires others to succeed. For many young women who have not known role models from their culture, it is crucial for them to know what I have overcome to be a successful educator. I feel a sense of obligation that by sharing my story, I am influencing young women to strive for higher levels in their career aspirations.

My collaborative style comes from learning to adapt and by accepting myself and my life experiences as integral to who I am as a leader. I believe that my ability to listen and to respect the perspectives of others helps me work in diverse settings and to challenge the conventional solutions to complex educational issues.

Did you have formal or informal mentors? If yes, how did they support you? In what ways did your gender or culture enhance or limit your access to mentoring?

I always had informal mentors. When it became apparent that mentoring was important for women and persons of color, I had already reached the level of principal, so I became a formal mentor for others. The Ford Foundation funded a University of Southern California (USC) led program with the goal of increasing Latino teachers by supporting Latino instructional aides in pursuing their college diplomas and teaching credentials. The findings from this work demonstrated that mentoring was a powerful component in the success of the participants. The support of family and colleagues was integral to goal attainment for the participants. Serving in an advisory role to this project, I realized that I had overcome significant traditional barriers without formal support from a mentoring system.

During this time, I helped launch the mentoring program for aspiring administrators started by the LAUSD Council of Mexican American Administrators. As a formal mentor, I was able to help women and other Latinos strive for advancement in the LAUSD promotional system. It was most gratifying helping others increase their personal qualities of leadership.

When I was president of the California Association of Latino Superintendents and Administrators (CALSA), I met Dr. Ken Magdaleno who was a graduate student working on research related to mentoring to increase the ranks of Latino administrators. His doctoral work became the foundation for one of the most successful mentoring programs for Latinos and women. I am currently mentoring a talented African American woman who is a successful principal and who aspires to become a superintendent.

What do you see as your strong personal qualities that helped you break through barriers to becoming a superintendent?

I believe that my ability to work effectively with diverse groups is one of my strongest attributes when thinking about the position of superintendent. I have worked in multiethnic settings successfully because I value what others bring to the conversation. My experiences as a child and later as a student taught me that there is great potential in others, and I have always felt that it was my role to draw out that potential.

My commitment to build on assets that others bring to the educational setting has opened doors of opportunity in bridging traditional divides. I thrive among diverse groups because I see myself as a representative of two cultures that enriched my life, and I am determined that children will also see themselves represented in our curriculum and in our classrooms. Being culturally mixed and growing up in the Latino culture has deepened my respect for all groups.

I also believe that my personal journey of overcoming barriers to success strengthened the tenacity needed to be an effective leader. Leadership is a roller coaster with times of great triumph and times of distress. Without tenacity and a strong moral compass, one could lose sight of the goal. My personal strength comes from within, and I hope to inspire others to find their potential.

Describe some of the important qualities for women (women of color) leaders in education.

Women in leadership roles have a unique opportunity to move the achievement agenda for all children. I believe that women who have overcome barriers to achieve the title of leader represent the commitment to the success of all children. Having others follow your lead is a great honor, and I believe that women must use the opportunity wisely. Women can have a powerful impact on classrooms, schools, and districts by bringing diverse groups together to work on ensuring the academic success of students of all ethnic backgrounds.

Women are good listeners, and they generally do not let their egos get in the way of what is best for schools, children, and the community. Women tend to be collaborative, and this quality allows them to bring everyone together around a common agenda.

What are some of the difficulties you have experienced as a woman of color administrator?

At times, I found that others wanted to define me as a Latina rather than a qualified administrator. I was proud to be Latino, but I wanted to be viewed as a leader who had succeeded based on merit. In the 1970s and 1980s, traditional leaders would often say that you got your job because you are Latino. I got my job because I worked hard and was competent, and this type of stereotyping was offensive to me and demeaning of the hard work of others like me. It always surprises me when comments are made about increased numbers of people of color at the leadership level. Few complaints occurred when district leaders were predominately represented by white individuals; however, when too many people of color advance to that level, questions surface regarding the shift in leadership.

My personal passion for helping English learners almost limited my access to the superintendency. Expertise in language acquisition should have defined me as a leader for all children, yet it was viewed as my entire expertise. I always caution women of color to not allow themselves to be defined by a single agenda.

How do women become identified with being in charge, without being identified with negative or unfeminine ways?

Women must not hesitate to show their strength in leadership roles. Women should know their personal compass well so that they are consistent in their focus and clearly articulate their passion for creating successful educational environments for all children. Others look for consistency in the behavior of their leaders, and not being clear about what you stand for is one of the reasons that others will not follow. It is better to have disagreement with your priorities than to be someone who wavers in her beliefs.

Leaders must respect the culture in which they work, building on what is in place. Women are uniquely qualified to be bridge builders because they tend to nurture change rather than forcing others to move to a new way of doing things. Top-down leadership can be viewed as disrespectful, and women who are in charge tend to understand the need to bring people together in consensus for long-term success. A woman should be clear that her qualities as a woman are assets, and it is not necessary to behave like a male to be viewed as a strong leader.

In what ways are the issues surrounding authority similar for a male and female leader, specifically women of color?

Male and female leaders share a common goal—to improve the educational outcomes for all children. How males and females approach moving toward this goal reflects their personal passions and, what I call, inner moral compasses. Leaders sacrifice on a personal level to be allowed to lead others. Women have the traditional challenges of balancing personal and professional lives, sustaining marriage and family, as they work long and arduous hours advancing their careers. Males have moved closer to the middle regarding family, yet they are viewed as being able to have a leadership role without family being viewed as a challenge. Societal values related to the role of women in leadership are changing; however, I find that the question of balance in one's personal life is one of the most frequently asked questions when I talk to women aspiring to become educational leaders.

Males and females must both make the tough calls and be willing to remain in the debate when it relates to students and their success. In this way, authority is similar and carriers the same burden of responsibility. Both males and females are held accountable for outcomes. Success is a hard fact, and women and men are equally measured by data. The story of how success is achieved is the richer story, yet the public's desire for quick fixes only looks at data. Males and females face the same harsh criticism and challenge of leading in increasingly demanding times. I believe that the conversations that are taking place around educational reform must bring male and female leaders together to share best practice and to support one another in climbing the achievement-gap hill.

Resource C

Maria G. Ott, PhD

Autobiography

An Unusual Journey

One of the unusual aspects of my life is the story of how a little girl, born in Germany to the son of Mexican immigrants and a German farm girl, came to become a spokesperson for language acquisition issues and a champion of educational opportunities for all children. My story and journey began in Kronach, Germany, where I was born. My father was stationed in Germany during the Occupation, and he found his soul mate on a farm in the country outside Kronach. This is the reason I started life on German soil and learned German as my first language. When my father secured approval from the military to bring his German war bride to California to live with his family in the barrios of East Los Angeles, I became a part of the Latino culture and family that were my father's pride.

My memories of the early years in Germany are filled with connections to my mother and grandmother. I still remember the tear-filled day we left on a train to Amsterdam to board the SS Rotterdam to travel to New York. From New York to Chicago and then to Los Angeles, we traveled on a flight that took us to a strange and frightening world filled with new languages and new cultures. This first journey helped develop early resilience that would remain with me for a lifetime.

Germany to East Los Angeles

I started school as a kindergartner at Gravois Avenue School in the Los Angeles Unified School District. During the first year in Los Angeles, we lived with my father's sister and her family in a small house in the Lincoln Heights area and later with my uncle and his family in the City Terrace area. When we moved on our own, I remember the struggle of becoming part of my father's large extended family that had come to California from Chihuahua, Mexico. My father's education ended at Belvedere Junior High School, when he graduated and moved on into his life. Without a high school diploma or career training, my father moved between jobs, finally, taking trade classes to become a barber.

The large extended Gutierrez family included seven uncles and one aunt. My father was the 21st child of Maria and Jose Gutierrez, who were migrant farm workers for part of the year. Nine of their children reached adulthood, and eight were alive when I was a young child. The children born in Mexico still preferred to speak in Spanish, and all the adult males had served in the U.S. Army during World War II. Their stories of bravery were told during family picnics, and I remember my mother telling us that my uncles had survived great hardships during the war. They all viewed themselves as proud American citizens, and they wore their service to the nation as demonstration that they were part of mainstream America. Their blue-collar jobs were symbols of their success. They were proud yet humble brothers connected by their story of survival and their pride in service to a nation that had not yet found connection to a growing population of Mexican Americans.

Coming to Los Angeles immersed me into the culture of the Gutierrez family, proud Mexican Americans who maintained their roots while embracing the culture of mainstream America. My greatest challenge as a child was to learn English so that I could crawl out of the darkness of classroom instruction that assumed that every child should come to school proficient in the English language. To say that the classroom was frightening is an understatement. Sitting each day waiting to understand the teacher laid the foundation of my passion for English learners and my tenaciousness about helping all children succeed. No child should experience what welcomed me to kindergarten—the realization there was something lacking, and the lacking element was in me. Language defines you as a child, yet I was made to feel that my home language was an impediment—a problem that needed fixing.

When I describe my language background, I acknowledge my German mother's tongue, my mastery of English, and my journey to speak Spanish to connect with my Mexican American roots. Crossing the waters from Germany to East Los Angeles was a perilous journey in many ways, yet the experiences of those early years clearly developed the tenacity and courage to lead and contribute to the improvement of public education.

Attending college was not part of the expectations laid by my parents. It was a priority to prepare to work and support myself. My parents' conservative religious values caused them to enroll me in Catholic schools early in my education. This was viewed as a way to keep me focused on my schoolwork. In elementary school, teachers would question my mother about why her daughter did not look like her. This was uncomfortable in an environment that encouraged students who were middle class and predominately white, not those who did not fit the norm.

High School and College

Catholic elementary schools launched their students into a tracked high school system. I spent long nights studying in seventh and eighth grade to try to catch up to the students who started school speaking English. When E. D. Hirsch, Jr. (1987) wrote *Cultural Literacy: What Every American Needs to Know,* he described the knowledge that culturally literate Americans possess. My early years were filled with learning to speak English as well as my native English-speaking peers and filling in cultural gaps because no one in my family had the mainstream American experience.

I was fortunate and ended up in the best classes with the best teachers. These teachers viewed me as talented, and they expected I would go to college. My English teacher Sister Redempta introduced me to English literature, poetry, and expository and creative writing. This is when I learned that English was more than diagramming sentences and writing reports. Sister Redempta taught me to love the English language and to use it as a tool for life.

By high school, I learned the rules and was navigating toward college. I met my future husband while attending high school, and he was a source of encouragement when I decided to apply to Mount St. Mary's College, in Los Angeles. Work-study programs and scholarships provided financial support, and working at secretarial jobs during summer and breaks helped pay the remaining tuition and living costs. I never considered a public college or university because the concept of attending a large school was too far out of my experience, and did not seem attainable.

Mount St. Mary's College has a long tradition of opening the doors of opportunity for minority women, especially Latinas. The school's success has earned the college a record of excellence for women breaking through the barriers of poverty and opening career opportunities. I consider the decision to attend Mount St. Mary's College life altering. My life was like a paper canoe sailing down the river of experience, and Mount St. Mary's turned that paper canoe into a well-armed warship ready to take on the challenges of a career, marriage, motherhood, and public service. I remember attending a church social event in high school. My father was to pick me up, and as he waited in the church parking lot, a group of young, white males insulted him by calling him a "beaner." My father was fuming when I came to the car. The restraint that he used in not starting a problem was a tribute to his desire to do what was best for his children. My blood boils every time that I think of that night. How dare anyone insult my hardworking father. Beaner was a term used to insult and let a Mexican American know how he or she was viewed. When I ask myself why I have such a sense of urgency about my work, I know that each experience left a mark. Most of life's day-to-day activities are easily forgotten, yet hurtful and embarrassing situations sting even in our senior years. We have the wisdom to understand ignorance, intolerance, and fear; however, the desire to prevent these hurtful experiences touching other lives seems only to grow stronger with age. I often ask myself if I will ever be able to let it go.

While I was at Mount St. Mary's College, the school transitioned from a two-semester to a trimester system. By carrying a full load during those years, I was able to accelerate my completion of graduation requirements, finishing one-third of the way into my senior year. I was married in the fall of my senior year, and I started working for an aerospace company as a receptionist in their personnel office.

I was perplexed during my first year out of college—what to do with the rest of my working life? As an English major at Mount St. Mary's College, I expected to teach high school English or to follow a career in journalism. Serving as an editor on the college newspaper, I learned to love the power of the printed word. Also, the idea of being a journalist that followed the highest ethical standards for reporting societal events appealed to my altruistic side—somehow I would help make a better world.

During my third year at Mount St. Mary's, I had the opportunity to take a teaching observation course. I was assigned to a school that served families living in the Brentwood area near UCLA. The sixth-grade class was in the process of producing one of Shakespeare's plays. All the students were fluent in English, and came from middle-class to high-income families. In fact, several well-known actors sent their children to this school. These were the preintegration days, and this school was a public school that felt like a private school. Want and hardship were not evident in the class that I observed for several weeks. This experience made we question whether I was suited to teaching. The students would do well whether I chose to follow the inner voice that said, "Be a teacher." This experience caused a tug and pull between teaching and journalism.

Early Married Life

After my marriage, my husband started teaching at a Catholic K–8 school while attending Loyola University to work on his master's degree in English. One of his students struggled with English. She was an eighth-grade immigrant in need of tutoring and English language instruction. My husband asked if I would help this student, and the experience was the cure for my dilemma regarding becoming a leader. I felt needed and rewarded by working with this young lady, and I became increasingly interested in my husband's experiences in the classroom.

My job opportunities included working for a newspaper in the garment industry. The starting pay for a journalist was $400 in 1969, and I needed to earn more than this to help with my share of the budget. Ending up in the personnel department of an aerospace company was not the vision I had for my career, yet it gave me some skills that have helped in my future leadership roles. I learned to be client-focused and customer friendly. When aerospace took a downturn during my first year of employment, the personnel office made major reductions to the staff, and I was reassigned to procurement. I learned to take and fill large aerospace orders that reached the million-dollar level. This experience taught me to be precise and to manage data.

Teaching Special Needs Students

Following my first year of employment, I received information from Mount St. Mary's that the Los Angeles Unified School District (LAUSD) was hiring teachers for special education. This was the only shortage field during a time of limited education hiring. Positions were available at the elementary and secondary level. Selected teacher applicants would have an intensive internship period while beginning coursework at Mount St. Mary's College to earn a special education credential. Interns would work under the direction of a master teacher for a semester, then they would be assigned to their classrooms throughout the LAUSD.

When I was interviewed, I described my experience helping the students at my former school, and I talked about the ESL student I tutored in my husband's class. The really big question was, Do you want to teach at secondary or elementary?

Since I was an English major who envisioned teaching the great works to high school students, I should have said that I wanted to work at secondary. Instead, I said I would work at the level that needed me the most, so I was assigned to the elementary level.

Prior to our student teaching assignments, we were placed on buses to tour the inner city of Los Angeles. This was where the need for teachers was greatest, and we were selected because we were a group of "making the world a better place" teacher candidates, and we were unafraid of poverty, racially segregated neighborhoods, or the challenges of addressing severe underperformance by students assigned to special education classrooms.

My first class was a span class with students at all elementary levels. The 18 students assigned to my class were predominantly Mexican American, and had a broad range of disabilities. I was disturbed that many of my students were labeled special education when their real need was for effective instruction to help them reach grade-level expectations in English. In 1975, PL 94–142 became effective, opening the door to better understanding of special education students' needs and appropriate intervention. There have been positives and negatives since passage of federal law to ensure that eligible students are appropriately educated. I witnessed firsthand students who were labeled inappropriately, and I taught my class, as if my students were gifted and talented, and they behaved like the best students in the entire school.

I asked the principal if I could work with my students in Spanish as preparation for Cinco de Mayo, a symbolic celebration of pride for Mexican Americans. The principal wanted to be supportive so he gave me permission to use Spanish but cautioned that I could only use Spanish for this assignment and activities. The students were so proud of their work in their native language. I could see great potential hidden under the label of low expectations by a system that did not know how to respond to a growing immigrant population.

In spring 1972, I read an announcement in the Los Angeles Unified School District (LAUSD) newsletter that there were openings in a bilingual program funded by federal Title VII resources. Teachers bilingual in Spanish could apply and would have to pass a proficiency test to demonstrate bilingual competence. I decided to apply and took the test receiving the highest ranking of A-level fluency in Spanish. I interviewed at three schools and received three employment offers. One of the schools was in my old neighborhood on the East side of Los Angeles. City Terrace Elementary School was my choice, and I was assigned to a second-grade classroom.

My leadership skills developed at City Terrace. Because bilingual education was new, responding to the *Lau v. Nichols*, 414 U.S. 563 (1974) decision resulting from a lawsuit filed in San Francisco on behalf of Chinese American students, the Title VII program in LAUSD was under a constant spotlight. It was common to have large groups of visitors walking through our classrooms, taking notes on our teaching strategies and materials. My students were mostly native speakers of English, and approximately half of them had family members who spoke Spanish in the home. We used a model that required daily teaching of English and Spanish reading. The professional development provided was extensive, and we had new resources to support our teaching.

At the end of my first year at City Terrace, my principal asked me to become a master teacher for student teachers from Cal State University at Los Angeles. This experience of having a student teacher each semester helped me become more reflective of my teaching practice since I needed to explain the decisions I made in the classroom to guide my student teachers to be well prepared to succeed to be well-prepared teachers.

In 1975, I had an opportunity to promote to a position of English as a Second Language/Gifted and Talented Education (ESL/GATE) coordinator at Sierra Vista Elementary School in the El Sereno area of Los Angeles. When I was selected, I knew that I would teach English on a pull-out and pull-in basis at all grade levels. I was also to work with the GATE students. I learned to stretch the potential of GATE students through differentiated instruction and attended the statewide conference for GATE, learning how I could become more effective in meeting the needs of this population. I knew that many of the most gifted students were at risk in the traditional classroom, and I made it a goal to learn how to be a voice for their special needs.

The two years that I spent at Sierra Vista prepared me to take on increasingly more complex and difficult challenges. I was the school translator for public meetings, and I was the direct support to classroom teachers for ESL students. My confidence continued to grow, and I was ready to accept an assignment as English/language arts adviser in fall of 1977. In this role, I worked with teachers throughout an area in LAUSD designated as Region G. The area encompassed East Los Angeles, and I worked on curriculum and professional development.

School Leadership as a Vice Principal

In fall of 1978, my former principal at Sierra Vista Elementary School was assigned as principal to Murchison Elementary School, serving the area that included the Ramona Gardens Housing Project. He asked that I be assigned as his vice principal. The need for a strong leadership team for Murchison was a priority for Region G Superintendent Bill Anton, and he made a special personnel assignment that allowed my appointment without the regular promotional exam process. I served as vice principal for more than three years, moving the school from traditional to year-round calendar, and improving achievement and student safety. In 1981, I took the principals exam and placed in the top 5%. The experiences of working in an area of high-crime statistics and at a low-achieving school serving many recent immigrants and students with high levels of poverty convinced me that leadership was essential to building a strong culture of teaching and learning. My principal was an outstanding instructional leader, and I learned about leadership under his mentorship. He taught me that the role of the principal was to keep focus, coherency, and priorities. I learned that it is not possible to do everything well, so I had to select the areas that make the greatest impact on the quality of teaching and learning to ensure that my efforts made a difference for students. Working under this mentor helped me become a strong principal.

Becoming a Principal

Working under this mentor (a white male) helped me become a strong principal. In 1981, I was assigned to be the principal of Hart Street School in Canoga Park. The staff was a veteran group of highly experienced teachers, and they were surprised to learn that their principal was young. At 32, I was much younger than the majority of the staff, and I worked hard to demonstrate my competence and to build positive relationships with the teachers. When I was assigned to Hart Street, the school had recently been identified as a participant in the LAUSD desegregation program. Although being designated as a Predominantly Hispanic, Black, and Other non-Anglo Minority (PHBAO) school brought additional resources to the school, not all teachers saw this as a benefit. Hart Street School was entering an era of new expectations and accountability, and teachers did not all agree with the focus on underperforming students, especially the focus on English learners who were a significant part of the Hispanic population.

Leading the Hart Street team to dedicate themselves to all students was my first most significant leadership challenge. The fact that the teachers viewed me as young and inexperienced led me to keep highly structured relationships with them so that they would have confidence in my ability to lead the school under the new PHBAO expectations. Even now, as superintendent, I look back fondly at this team of veteran educators who made me demonstrate that I could lead with passion and commitment.

During my second year as principal, my area superintendent nominated me for outstanding principal as part of a Los Angeles Chamber of Commerce recognition program. I was embarrassed to be nominated since I believed that I had not yet earned this honor. And following this recognition, I received a requested transfer to a school closer to home. The transfer caused mixed feelings, as I had become deeply attached to the Hart Street staff and community. We were working as a team, and together, we were pushing a rigorous academic agenda for all students.

When I arrived at my second assignment as elementary principal, I drove around the school and community to get a flavor for the neighborhood. Poverty was evident on every block. Sheridan Street School was covered with graffiti and looked neglected. In my first weeks at the school, I learned that my office manager had retired and that several top staff members were planning to leave. I had been assigned to a school in crisis, giving me the opportunity to demonstrate that I was the leader worthy of the outstanding principal nomination bestowed on me by my former area superintendent.

The school board member who represented Sheridan Street School dropped by for an unannounced visit during my first weeks at the school to let me know that he expected me to move the school forward and to be responsive to the community and staff. He wanted someone who was a Latina and who could speak Spanish. When he was told that I met both requirements, he wanted to come see for himself. This was my first encounter with the politics of school boards. After several years at Sheridan, this same board member would compliment me repeatedly on the great job I was doing in leading the school. I believe that the rapport that I built with the community was more than a reflection of my ethnicity and Spanish-language abilities. This rapport was built on the day-to-day hard work of addressing the problems and creating long-term solutions.

I had only been the principal at Sheridan for two years when I was offered the opportunity to take a promotional assignment as a director of instruction for another area of the school district. After giving the offer a thorough review, I declined the promotion. My belief was that someone leading instruction for other principals should have demonstrated that she could move a school to new levels of achievement. Colleagues and supervisors told me that I had made an error in turning down this opportunity—one does not turn down a promotion. I still find it interesting that I was not commended for wanting to become a stronger leader before promoting. Although I had been a principal for four years, I had not been at one school long enough to demonstrate the outcomes of my instructional leadership.

PhD Candidate and District-Level Leader

While still principal at Sheridan Street School, I was selected to enter the doctoral program at the University of Southern California (USC). The USC doctoral program stretched my expertise and broadened my ability to provide instructional leadership. As a member of a cohort, I also developed professional friendships with doctoral students who were outside of LAUSD. It was beneficial for my later career choices to expand my horizons and to establish mentors and contacts in the broader educational arena. Three years of rigorous coursework at USC deepened my knowledge about effective instructional practice and about the role of policy in setting agendas for educating all students.

I have never regretted the decision to pass on my first promotional opportunity since the additional three years as principal at Sheridan led the school to new heights of effectiveness. When the second promotion was offered, I accepted the role as administrator for the Eastman Curriculum Design Project, which had started as a research-based design at Eastman Elementary School and was expanded to 28 schools.

Bilingual Leader

The Eastman Project placed me in the center of districtwide efforts since the 28 schools were spread across the district. The visibility of the training and research aspects of the program allowed me to demonstrate leadership and enhanced by career opportunities within LAUSD. The positive academic achievement outcomes of the Eastman project as well as the growing controversy around bilingual education as a method to address a growing population of nonnative speakers of English in U.S. public schools brought national attention.

The 28 Eastman schools were divided into two groups—the seven project schools that were part of the research component and that received intensive training and the 20 expansion schools that volunteered to participate in the training with the goal of replicating the outcomes from Eastman Elementary School. The 28 schools developed camaraderie and support for one another, and they were considered on the forefront of effective reform for schools serving large populations of English learners.

Principals who worked in these schools were strong leaders who were willing to organize their schools in a way that would change the paradigm for teaching and learning in bilingual settings.

During this period, the federal funding that supported some of the training through a Title VII grant was ending, so a dissemination grant was developed. This grant was successful, and the Eastman Curriculum Design project became a national project. Under the new role, the Eastman project was called Model Organizational Results of Eastman or Project M.O.R.E. Being associated with a program that produced such outstanding outcomes for students and promised to guide school leaders to rethink ineffective bilingual models was a highlight in my career.

One unique role that came to me during my Eastman project assignment was the opportunity to debate issues related to language policy. I found myself opposite U.S. English on cable television discussing the merits of educating students through their primary language to reach high levels of English success. The courage to confront controversy on behalf of children reflected my personal journey.

When I was promoted to the position of administrator for the language acquisition and bilingual development branch in 1989, I had the pleasure of working with an outstanding leader who would become a mentor throughout my career. Amelia McKenna was the assistant superintendent, and as a Latina who grew up in the Wilmington area of Los Angeles, she fully understood the importance of effectively educating the district's growing population of English learners. She was a powerful leader for language development, and she refused to allow programs serving English learners to be second class in their importance for LAUSD. Together, we fought to implement programs that would help students achieve high levels of English.

Little Lake City Schools and the Importance of District Size

In 1993, I received a call from my mentor encouraging me to apply for the superintendent vacancy in the Little Lake City School District. The district was small, serving 5,400 students in the cities of Santa Fe Springs, northern Norwalk, and southeastern Downey. My first reaction to this encouragement was that I could not see myself as a superintendent, and I certainly did not see myself leaving my career in LAUSD. In retrospect, I realize that my reluctance to being open to this opportunity was born from my fear of not being worthy. When children grow up in disadvantaged circumstances, they carry self-doubts. Although I had a successful career, I questioned whether I could be an effective superintendent. This self-doubt was a remnant of my early struggles to learn English and do well in school.

After resisting the encouragement to apply, I was told that going through the process would be a good experience because the process would help clarify whether this was a career move that would be right for me. I submitted the application for the position on the last possible day, delivering the documents to the home of the search consultant. The courage to take this first step came from somewhere deep within, from the encouragement of my mentor, and from my husband who thought this would be a good opportunity to use the education I received in the doctoral program at USC. When one says that things work out for a reason, I think that describes my journey from LAUSD to the Little Lake City School District—a match that was destined to take place.

The Little Lake City School District provided the experiences that would launch my leadership as a superintendent of schools. The board reflected the student makeup, with two Anglo board members and three Latino board members. Coming from LAUSD, I was accustomed to a high level of expertise at the staff level. In small districts, staff members function as generalists, and they do not reach the level of technical knowledge needed in a district like LAUSD. At my first principals meeting in Little Lake, the principals sat around a conference table. My adjustment to this change from being in the second-largest district in the nation to being in a district with nine schools took a long time. First, I realized that I needed to learn the culture of Little Lake so I could effectively lead the district to realize its potential. In turn, the district needed to adjust to the fact that their leader was coming from a district not known for having a collaborative culture. The challenge of winning over the staff and community polished my leadership skills to new levels.

When Little Lake hired me, the trustees established a goal of unifying the district, which would have required an election to move Santa Fe High School in the Whittier Union High School District under their governance structure. Students from Little Lake moved on to Santa Fe High School in the high school district. The board indicated that I would have a year to become grounded in the district then I could begin the work of leading the district and community toward a unification vote. The superintendent of the high school district was an experienced educator, and he moved his most talented administrator into the position of principal at the high school to undermine any efforts to unify.

I moved the unification study into a strategy within our Little Lake strategic plan and started to study the issue. The high school principal and two of her teachers were participants in the action team to investigate how to improve K–12 articulation. The yearlong study included participants from the community and staff representatives from Little Lake and the three high school representatives. Many difficult discussions occurred around what was needed to improve articulation and impact student achievement, and the group studied all research available on district configurations. We learned that articulation did not automatically improve because a district was organized as a unified system. Many of the unified districts we studied had limited articulation. We also found outstanding articulation in some systems that worked intentionally to maintain high levels of articulation between elementary districts and a high school district.

It was clear that focused intent was needed to connect systems and that organizational structures alone did not ensure effective cross-level working relationships on behalf of improved student achievement. The interesting outcome of this effort was that I worked with the high school superintendent to submit a grant to the Annenberg Foundation as part of the LA Annenberg project to reform public education. Our successful effort produced a $1.25 million grant to connect the educational program in literacy and mathematics.

The outcomes from our academic articulation and cross-system staff development efforts produced improved achievement for students across Little Lake and at Santa Fe High School.

My experience in Little Lake also taught me that size and stability matter when working to reform education. Little Lake had a stable history at the superintendent level, demonstrated by the 12-year tenure of my predecessor. In contrast to large, urban systems that are characterized by frequent leadership changes, it was expected that a leader would stay to carry out the vision and mission established by the school board. The seven years that I led Little Lake City Schools taught me that size does matter. It is not a guarantee of success; however, it does make the work of closing achievement gaps and building a culture of commitment to the needs of all children more attainable.

LAUSD and Changing the Paradigm of Urban Education

While working with the boards of education for both districts to enter into a Memorandum of Understanding to ensure the continuity of our efforts beyond the life of the grant, I received a call from LAUSD in June 2000. The caller was from the superintendent's office, inquiring whether I would be interested in talking to Roy Romer, the new superintendent in LAUSD, about working as his deputy to implement the redesign plan developed under interim superintendent Ramon Cortines. The plan was titled *Eleven Local Districts, One Mission: A Multiple District Plan for Transforming the Los Angeles Unified School District*. Clearly, the invitation was enticing; however, I was in the middle of the Annenberg effort to connect Little Lake and Santa Fe High School, and I envisioned that my next career move would be to lead a larger school district. I asked myself whether I could be the second in authority and work to implement someone else's vision for the future. This was a perplexing opportunity.

Mentors have always helped me with difficult decisions. And I was part of the national group of Annenberg superintendents and valued the advice of these colleagues. We had a meeting in June 2000, where I was able to seek the advice of colleagues who encouraged me to accept the position.

The work in LAUSD was perhaps the most challenging of my career. As a nontraditional superintendent, the LAUSD board required that Roy Romer find an educational deputy to help him run the district. I accepted the deputy position with the commitment that

I would do everything possible to help Romer succeed as superintendent. I remembered how difficult it had been for Leonard Britton to succeed when he assumed the LAUSD superintendent's position in July 1987. Coming from outside the system presented unique challenges for any new superintendent. My gift to Romer was my unwavering loyalty.

During this time in my career, I was considered an experienced superintendent, and I had held leadership positions in statewide organizations. Returning to LAUSD was both a positive career decision and also a negative because I passed on the opportunity of leading in my own right with my vision and ability to influence educational outcomes for all children.

During the five years I spent as Romer's senior deputy superintendent, I learned about the power of clear communication and the power of weaving stories into your message to create images that help people understand your intent. Romer was a skilled communicator, and he was a strong leader who drove his agenda through a centralized approach. It was my role to help the organization move forward with Romer's priorities. Fortunately, Romer made instruction his priority. Early in his superintendency, we discussed the legacy he hoped to leave. His aspiration was to leave a legacy of improved instruction. I explained that to accomplish lasting instructional change in LAUSD, he would have to commit to more than three years. I stayed with Romer for five years, and he remained an additional year, serving more than six years as superintendent.

When I evaluate the decision to join Romer, I am convinced that I made the right decision. I learned why large urban districts struggle to improve. The lack of sustained reform efforts and the lack of stable leadership contribute to a self-fulfilling culture of failure. Working with central and local leadership to improve literacy, academic achievement, and graduation rates was a rewarding role during the Romer superintendency, and I strengthened my tenacity, political skills, and ability to influence people. When I returned to the position of superintendent, I was a much more skilled leader.

In 2005, I received a call from recruiters to apply for superintendent of the Rowland Unified School District. This call came at a time when I was ready to consider returning to the role of superintendent because of the major changes that were occurring in LAUSD that made efforts to sustain reforms increasingly difficult. In 2004, two of the LAUSD reform-minded school board members were unseated. The outcome of the board election was another reconfiguration of the district's structure. Three of the eleven local district administrative structures were eliminated in a short period. What was described as a strategy for reducing costs resulted in minimal budget savings and caused great disruption to the three impacted communities. The most disheartening outcome of the change was that staff that believed that LAUSD was not capable of sustaining reform could point to the rapid change as evidence that the if you wait long enough reforms disappear for lack of support. My application to Rowland Unified was successful, and I was appointed superintendent in July 2005.

When I left LAUSD, Romer told me I was the glue for the system. This compliment was affirmation of my role in supporting him during five exciting and difficult years. Romer was a leader who encouraged his team to take risks and pursue opportunities, and he was pleased that I was moving to a district that would enhance my career. I left LAUSD with new awareness of my unique talents, and my influence on the positive changes that occurred in LAUSD during my tenure as senior deputy superintendent continue to reinforce that I made the right decision when I accepted Romer's offer. I also left with a heavy heart and increased awareness that urban education is vulnerable to instability that undermines the trust needed to create a great system.

Rowland Unified: The Leader as Transformer

Starting as superintendent in Rowland Unified in 2005, the first order of business was to listen and learn the culture of my new district while building relationships with staff and the community. The superintendent's cabinet included four assistant superintendents with extensive careers in the district. The least veteran member of the cabinet had more than 10 years in the district. The other three had been in the district more than 30 years. This experienced team could have made my transition difficult; however, I found a group of dedicated individuals who would help me during my first 90 days and beyond. They advised me on the traditions of the Rowland Unified School District and helped me analyze the needs of the district.

I was hired by a board that was stable and committed to the children of the community. One of their major concerns was the loss of students under a 1994 state law that authorized districts by board resolution to become Districts of Choice. Few districts had opted for this strategy because interdistrict transfer laws met the needs of most districts and produced a collaborative relationship related to the movement of students between districts. However, Rowland Unified was the district most impacted by the District of Choice law.

District of Choice ignited my passion for social justice. This law was cloaked in the good intentions of giving parents an opportunity to select schools for their children, unconstrained by traditional district boundaries. Diane Ravitch (2010) addresses the problems with choice in *The Death and Life of the Great American School System: How Testing and Choice Are Undermining Education.* Her compelling arguments could have been written about the impact of District of Choice on Rowland Unified.

I found myself the spokesperson for the ills of District of Choice. Through frequent testimony before the legislature, I realized that public policy is subject to politics. As superintendent, it was my role to lead my district to continue to distinguish itself as an exemplary school system and to demonstrate that Rowland schools were the best choice for families living within our boundaries while continuing to work with members of the legislature to amend the flaws in the District of Choice law.

Racism in the 21st century is more subtle than when I experienced it as a child. Well-intentioned public officials are vulnerable to creating short-term solutions to the complex challenges of educating all children to their potential, preventing and closing achievement gaps. The opportunity to participate in rigorous educational experiences is described as a civil right, yet the abandonment of neighborhood schools under the guise of parental choice leaves far too many students behind.

In Rowland Unified, the environment for improving the conditions for socioeconomically disadvantaged students as well as for English learners provided the context for change. A culture of trust was emerging with teachers who demonstrated a willingness to work in collaborative ways to raise expectations and produce improved results. In 2005, Rowland Unified was identified as one of three outlier districts by Pivot Learning (formerly Springboard Schools), defying the odds by producing positive academic results for its diverse student population. That same year, the Ball Foundation headquartered in Glen Ellen, Illinois, invited Rowland Unified to apply for a partnership grant to improve literacy for all students. The selection process was national, and Rowland Unified applied, starting a long-term partnership with one of the most innovative foundations in the nation.

The Ball Foundation was founded in 1975 by G. Carl Ball and his wife Vivian. Carl Ball served as CEO of Ball Horticultural, one of the largest producers of commercial seed for flowers and ornamental plants. Carl Ball was a successful businessman who believed that public schools were not fulfilling their mission. When his wife challenged him to do something about his concerns, he decided to serve as a substitute teacher in West Chicago. The experience was transformative, and Carl Ball decided to place some of his wealth into an educational foundation to develop models of excellence for high levels of achievement in literacy. His vision of creating systems that worked for all children distinguished this amazing man for his generosity and belief in the potential of teachers and of all children.

Rowland Unified was selected as a finalist in 2006 and entered the design phase for partnering with the Ball Foundation. During the 2006–2007 school year, the Ball consultants conducted a survey of Rowland's assets to ensure that district leadership was aware of the strengths within the district. These assets were used as the foundation for beginning work with staff and the community. In 2007, the assets were woven into the data analysis conducted during strategic planning. The development of the Rowland Strategic Plan was comprehensive, involving a broad-based group to set the framework. Known as the Rowland Core Team, the group represented all stakeholders, and the mission, parameters, objectives, and strategies shaped by this group were approved by the school board. For approximately eight months, teams of teachers, classified staff, parents, high school students, and community members met every Wednesday night to develop eight strategies into action plans that would lead the district to realize its mission statement.

Since July 2008, the partnership work with the Ball Foundation included the work defined in the Rowland Strategic Plan and Ball Partnership Agreement, including professional growth activities mutually developed to improve teaching and learning. During the fiscal crisis in California, school districts were forced to eliminate crucial support for professional growth, and Rowland was uniquely positioned to continue improving student achievement through a strategy of collaboration that focused on best teaching practices and on high expectations for students and teachers. This work has been personally gratifying, watching schools reach new levels of excellence and earn state and national recognition.

I continue to be struck by how some people want little to do with children of poverty, and this is most evident in the national debate around parental choice. Rowland Unified is a place that is demonstrating that a system that is diverse, both in ethnicity and in socioeconomic levels, can demonstrate high levels of success for all children. In *All Systems Go: The Change Imperative for Whole System*

Reform, Michael Fullan (2010) describes the importance of the school system in supporting school improvement. On page 56, he mentions that Rowland Unified is one of these places.

During the years of working with the Ball Foundation, teacher leaders in Rowland Unified have emerged to shape three powerful strands that are transforming the school district. Teachers who participate in Communities of Practice meet in person and online to share best practices around key learning questions. Teachers work with administrators and classified staff to shape system-level efforts to improve student achievement in the instructional cabinet. And teacher leaders and administrators meet together to learn how to use efficacious practices to transform teaching and learning through the school instructional leaders strand. This work has reinforced my belief that collaboration is the only sustainable path to transformation of public education.

Reflections

Remembering my humble beginnings, I continue to believe that I have a perspective about the achievement gap that enriches my effectiveness as a leader. I have benefited from supportive mentors, male and female, who have helped me realize my potential. In looking back on my unusual journey, I cannot forget that a child is shaped by environment, by the love and support of parents, by adversity when coupled with opportunity for growth, and by the kindness of teachers, administrators, and other supportive adults.

My journey is far from over. My husband and I have been married for 41 years, and we are now the grandparents of five beautiful granddaughters and one grandson. I know that leaders who have a fire inside for making a difference for all children need to continue to influence others so that public education learns from misguided policies and failed attempts at reform. Sustainability of effort is only possible by the commitment and perseverance of educators who want only one outcome—that every child will succeed. I hope that I contribute to this goal in my current role as superintendent and through my work with those I mentor.

Resource D

Darline P. Robles, PhD

Response to Guiding Questions

What are some of the life experiences you have had that facilitated your choice to become an educational leader?

As a young student, I moved to different schools in my elementary years, and as I got older, I realized that there were teachers who I connected with because they developed a relationship with me, but more often, teachers did not take the time to get to know me. I realized that as an individual and, eventually, as a teacher, that building relationships with people whom I worked with was critical. As a leader, I knew that I could create that type of environment, not only in my classroom, but also at a school level and a systems level. Creating an environment where everyone felt supported and challenged to their best has been my goal as leader. And my early school experiences taught me how important it is to be in a supportive and caring environment to succeed. My home environment was very caring and supportive and even though school and work life are not home, I firmly believe that those same places should be ones that allow for individuals to be creative to allow for maximum learning opportunities, but also for greater work production.

Describe ways you have achieved equitable recognition, visibility, opportunities, identity formation, and balance in your personal and professional life.

I have always been the type of individual who is willing to speak up about an issue I care about. Because of this personality trait, recognition and visibility, both good and bad, come to me naturally. As a young student, I would be the one to speak up on situations I felt were unfair to me or others; as a teacher, I would be the one to question a direction or policy by the administration. When I was at University of Southern California in the teacher corps program, I and about 10 others confronted the administration over the direction of the program. All of us were willing to make demands we felt would benefit us professionally, but as important, would benefit our community. At the end of six months, of an adversarial relationship with the administration, we were asked to leave the university. Through our actions, our professional identity was formed: We would fight for access and equity, not only for ourselves but for our community.

Describe the day you decided you wanted to become a school leader.

I can't recall a specific day, but I recall one day when my principal stated he did not want me to leave the classroom and take on a special assignment position at the district office. I was so upset that one individual could make that decision for me that could affect my professional growth. That was when I realized that could never happen again. I was committed to making sure that I was in control of my professional growth, and to do that, I must be in the role of a leader. Later on, when I worked at the district office and worked with principals, I realized how important the role of principal was in determining the culture and academic goals of a school. I then decided this is a position I wanted.

In what ways did your gender enhance or limit access to your early leadership roles?

I have never seen my gender as limiting. But I am keenly aware that others may treat me differently because I am a woman. My attitude has always been to move forward and not dwell on the different expectations or behaviors toward me. I know it is still a "man's world" in many respects and I may have to work twice as hard to prove myself to some people, but I have never seen that as limiting. I have always been self-confident and I see challenges as opportunities for personal growth.

How did your culture enhance or limit access to your early leadership roles?

Growing up during the 1960s and 1970s when Chicano pride was our goal, I believe made it easier to view my culture as an asset. Because

I was bilingual and bicultural, many in my district saw me as an asset to the district and looked to me to provide leadership in specific areas: multicultural education, English as a Second Language training, and parent education. Once the administration observed me in these settings, they realized I could do more, and I was given additional responsibilities to demonstrate my leadership skills. Early in my career, I understood the need for equity to meet the needs of underserved populations. My personal background and cultural experiences have been assets as I have advocated for equity and social justice.

Describe the role of mentors at this stage in your career.

I was fortunate to have strong Latina women as mentors early in my career, especially Dr. Mary Gonzales Mend. I had many strong women leaders at my school and also great men who guided me and taught me through their modeling and support. But Dr. Mend was the only one who was specific in her mentoring. She spent time with me, giving direct support, coaching, encouragement, and training on becoming a school leader. The day I decided to apply to become a superintendent, Dr. Mend provided me with a toolbox of materials to assist me with the interview process, resume writing, and everything I needed to prepare for the application process and final interview.

What do you see as your strong personal qualities that helped you in your initial leadership position?

My strongest personal qualities are interpersonal skills. Again, I believe you must connect with the people around you—even if they don't want to connect with you. As a teacher leader, bilingual coordinator, and elementary principal, I had to work with many individuals who did not want to change their instructional strategies to meet the changing student demographics. To move the staff in each of these settings, I had to build a relationship and provide a supportive environment, where they would be willing to try new behaviors and meet the student needs. Another personal quality is demanding the best from me and from others on behalf of all students and having high standards for everyone in the profession. And I have integrity. And I usually stay very calm under stressful situations. A newscaster once asked me if I was a Marine. He had just seen me be grilled by elected officials, and I responded to each question in a calm and respectful manner. He told me that he was in awe by my calmness, and thought I had to be a Marine to have remained so calm. I am also persistent in achieving my goals.

Did you have formal or informal mentors? If yes, how did they support you? In what ways did your gender or culture enhance or limit your access to mentoring?

I have been fortunate to have many mentors—both informal and formal. Part of my personality is to seek out individuals who have the skills and talents I need to build in myself. When I find that individual, I ask for his help. I am not afraid of asking for help. In one way, I think my gender has been an asset in accessing mentoring. I just think men are more hesitant to ask for help than women. As for my culture, I don't think it has limited my access to mentoring.

What do you see as your strong personal qualities that helped you break through barriers to becoming a superintendent?

An additional personal quality that was not mentioned previously is my willingness to take risks. If I had been timid or averse to risks, I would never have been willing to become the interim superintendent in Montebello USD. When I was asked to take this position, the district was close to being taken over by the state, and we had to cut more than 30% of the budget to survive. My willingness to take this on, as my first superintendency, demonstrates my courage and risk-taking qualities. Describe some of the important qualities for women (women of color) leaders in education.

Women leaders bring a new dimension to leadership through their natural collaborative style, great listening skills, empathy and willingness to see both sides of an issue, and work toward a win-win solution. Not to say that men don't do that, but women leaders seem to do it more naturally. Once women leaders take on an administrative position, they seem to stay longer in the position than men do. I believe this "staying power" and willingness to stay for the long haul is more evident in women leaders despite other professional growth opportunities.

What are some of the difficulties you have experienced as a woman of color administrator?

Some people have underestimated me, and had low expectations of my work. That more than anything has annoyed me. When I accomplished something, some people seemed to be surprised, as if I, a Latina, could not do it. This reaction has made me angry at times, but it has also energized me to do more and prove them wrong.

How do women become identified with being in charge, without being identified with negative or unfeminine ways?

You just lead. I don't think you can worry about how you will be identified or you will be stuck and not move forward. People will always have an opinion about you, whether that opinion is based on facts. As a leader, you must be who you are and be authentic. As for being feminine, there is nothing wrong with being who you are and still be in charge. Everyone's unique personalities and qualities will determine their success. *In what ways are the issues surrounding authority similar for a male and female leader, specifically women of color?*

Anyone in authority will have issues around control and power or how we use the position. It is up to the leader, male or female, to understand that real authority comes when you give it away, and it ensures that everyone in your organization feels ownership and responsibility for the success of the organization. I don't see it different for women of color—only that we are always in a fishbowl. We will often be the first Latina in the position, and others will see us as representing all women of color, so the issue is our success determines the access women have into leadership roles.

Resource E

Darline P. Robles, PhD

Autobiography

Early Life

I will always be thankful to my mother for being my first teacher and instilling in me the desire to always do my best. My mother taught me to read early, and I was allowed to enter kindergarten earlier than most students, at the age of four.

By the time I was in fourth grade, I attended several elementary schools in Montebello, East Los Angeles (ELA), and Pico Rivera. Moving to different elementary schools taught me the importance of developing relationships, how to quickly read people and my environment, and how to adapt to new situations and to be flexible—skills that would become extremely helpful to me later on in life.

Elementary School Years

Living in a single-parent home with a working mother gave me many opportunities to demonstrate my independence. My personal drive for success came from my mother's high expectations for me and from seeing my mother working while raising her children and being independent.

I had tremendous and unconditional love and support from my mother and a very large extended family that supported all of us. One can never underestimate the value of unconditional love and support that communicates to children that we believe in them, in their dreams, and in their ability to achieve their dreams if they work hard, while knowing we are there to support them. The belief in one's self and the confidence of knowing that one is safe and loved for who she is was the grounding that I needed, and other children need, to successfully meet and navigate the challenges of growing up.

One such challenge that had a great impact on me occurred when I was in sixth grade. I was passed over for the important recognition of leading a sixth-grade May Day event. The competition involved three top students giving a speech. The three students were Sandra, a Caucasian student, Janet, a Japanese student, and me. Even though many told me that I had done the best job, I was not selected. I was stunned. It was my first school experience of rejection, and I felt it was based on my color, not on merit. The confidence that had been instilled in my ability and me did not shake my sense of self-worth. It was clear to me that not being selected to lead the May Day event was not based on ability. It was based on color. I can recall this as if it were yesterday, and this definitely influenced my teaching experiences.

Junior High School Years

In junior high school, I had close friends from different cultural backgrounds, and again, I observed different treatment of students based on cultural background, socioeconomics, and language. I realized that students who did not speak English were sent to certain classrooms in the school, and basically, they were ignored and did not mingle with other students. I realized that to make it in junior high, you had to fit in and "hang" with certain groups or be called names. In my case, even though I spoke English and did fit in, it was confusing for me to hear my peers making pejorative comments about people who looked like me and people in my family. Somehow, what was communicated to me was it was bad to be Mexican. As I look back on this experience, I know this influenced both my teaching and administrative styles to ensure that all students felt cared for, honored for who they are, and respected for what they bring to their learning.

High School Years

In the ninth grade, our family moved to South El Monte, which required me to attend another school where I would have to learn to fit in. An aunt of mine was attending Sacred Heart of Mary (SHM) in

Montebello, and that seemed like a better alternative to me, so with the help of my father, who convinced my mother, I applied, and was accepted into the college-prep program. I didn't know what that meant until I started school in late January. I found out that there were three educational tracks at SHM. Fortunately, I made friends quickly and got involved in choir and other school activities. Again, I observed students being treated differently based on which tracks they were enrolled in (general, business, and college-prep), which also coincided with their ethnicity and socioeconomic status. Even though the nuns were not too kind to me, I decided to stay at SHM since I had very close friends at the school. By my sophomore year, I realized I should have left. The nuns were still treating those of us who did not live in Montebello or Monterey Park as students who were less worthy of their attention. In fact, I was the only girl in the college-prep program from ELA and not from Montebello, and they did not let me forget it. One experience I remember helped me get through it. I got to know a good friend who was living at Maryvale, an orphanage for girls in Rosemead. As I got to know her and learned about her background, I realized I was fortunate to have so much in my life when others had so little. Because I was strong and confident, because I had the confidence and support of my family and friends, I knew I could make it, regardless of how others were treating me. No matter what, I knew who I was, even though others tried to ignore me or overlook my strengths and talents. I was proud to be able to take the negative treatment of me and turn it into an opportunity to reinforce my strength.

College Years

Upon entering college, I had an interest in three careers, a lawyer, a psychologist, and a teacher. Right after high school, I was hired as a playground assistant director for Pico Rivera Parks and Recreation. I was assigned to Pio Pico Elementary School. This neighborhood was known for its poverty and very gang-involved families. Children who attended Pio Pico were known as troublemakers, and when I was hired, I was told that I probably could not get them involved in the many activities offered to the children through Parks and Recreation. When I began working in the summer, I was very excited about developing a great summer program. The director at the site allowed me to create the program to fit the needs of the community (e.g., sport, crafts, field trips, anything that would bring the kids to the playground from 10 a.m. to 6 p.m. every day). The children came every day and participated in all the activities, and that was when I realized I really wanted to teach. During the next several years at Pio Pico Parks and Recreation, the program was known as one of the best in the city. It was a program where the children felt they belonged, they felt cared for, and they felt success every day they participated in the program. I learned that with the right motivation and program elements, all children will participate and learn. I knew that I had had a hand in developing the success of the program and in making a difference in the lives of the children who participated in the program. It was one of the best jobs I ever had.

Having learned so much from my mother, being a good student myself, and wanting success for students like me and the ones I was working with at Pio Pico shaped my decision to become a teacher.

Marriage

In 1967, I met my future husband, and in 1969, we were married. By 1969, I left my job at the playground and focused on completing my studies. During this time, my husband Frank supported my decision to continue attending school, even though it would be harder once my son was born in 1970. In 1972, I finally achieved my goal, and received a BA in history, and now, I was determined to get my elementary credential. Finances prevented me from thinking about a master's degree, but in time, I heard about the support provided for students entering the Teacher Corps program at the University of Southern California (USC). Since my husband was the only one working, and because I did not want to apply for loans, I would need some kind of assistance to continue my studies. In June 1972, I was accepted into the Teacher Corps program at USC. At the end of the two years, I would earn a master's degree in urban education and a teaching credential.

Teacher Corp/Los Padrinos

During the summer and fall, I worked in Pasadena doing fieldwork and taught at Los Padrinos Juvenile Hall and Bunch Junior High in Compton. Many of the Chicanos in the program, including myself, were interested in working in bilingual settings or English as a second language (ESL) classes as part of our experience. However, we were told by the program administrators that they did not see the importance of such a focus. We were shocked by the response.

We tried to get local, state, and national support for our concerns but to no avail. Our demonstrations in front of the dean's office did not make an impact. Nine of us decided to leave the program, with some of us eventually completing our studies at Claremont Graduate School, which offered the best options for us. We fought for recognition of our culture and identity, and we took a stand. This same issue has come up several times in my career, of course, with different details. But the questions are always the same: Who are we? Are we recognized for who we are, and what do we stand for? Do we settle for less? These questions and the pursuit of just answers to them were and are driving forces in my life. The dogged pursuit of educational equity and social justice has a price. Trying to do the right thing for the right kids can take time and effort away from tending to one's family, and it can jeopardize professional aspirations if organizational leaders do not agree with one's equity agenda. Balancing the demands of one's personal convictions with one's professional goals is a challenge. But at the end of the day, who are we as family members, and as professionals, if we are not better individuals ourselves for making the world a better place for those whose voices are not heard and needs are not recognized in schools and in society?

New Teacher

I began teaching in the Montebello Unified School District (MUSD) at Montebello Intermediate School. Accepting the position at Montebello Intermediate was one of the best career choices I have made. Montebello Intermediate School embraced a student-centered culture and proved to have the best administrative team. It embraced teacher and parent involvement, encouraged creativity among its staff, and allowed many of us to attend outstanding professional development to increase our capacity to become better educators. Little did I know that one of the best mentors to shape my future career choices would be my principal, Mr. Nicholas Mansour.

Mentors

A key decision that Mr. Mansour made was to assign Momoyo Iwata as my team member in my first teaching assignment. Although

I found much support from colleagues, I know that without Momoyo's support during my first years of teaching, I would not have advanced in my career as quickly as I did. Momoyo was an outstanding teacher with much experience, but more important was her willingness to take the time to teach me. We taught in a large open classroom with about 40 students each. We planned together, and Momoyo was able to observe my teaching from her classroom, and would critique my lesson and give me tips on discipline and instructional strategies. These tips would have taken me years to learn, but by the end of my first year, I felt like a pro. This could not have happened without Momoyo spending the time with me after school and on the weekends to teach me. From conversations with Momoyo, I learned the importance of our life and cultural experiences on how we learn, teach, and lead. I learned the importance of allowing students to have choice and more freedom in their learning, but I also learned how to provide a structure to make those choices meaningful. From then on, I would plan my lessons differently to better meet my student's needs. Again, without Momoyo's guidance and her willingness to spend the time with me, I don't know when I would have had the aha moment. This first experience taught me the importance of being open to others' constructive criticism and advice. It also taught me the importance of using one's experience and expertise not to elevate one's position but to mentor others and give back to those new to the profession, whether they be teachers or new administrators in your school or district.

Early in my career, I found support and recognition from my peers and supervisors. The administrative team at Montebello Office of Instruction (MOI) (the school district is Montebello Unified School District, Montebello, California) was in my classroom on a regular basis and provided me with the feedback for growth. I took advantage of every professional development opportunity. I took leadership assignments, worked in the afternoon with English learners, and was able to provide professional development on ESL strategies to teachers. I became very involved with the parent council, and supported efforts to provide training to our parents.

After a few years, I was able to help implement the district's first bilingual/bicultural program for sixth to eighth grade. Around this time, I accepted a special assignment at the central office working with the coordinator of bilingual education. As a young Latina working with mostly white administrators, now at the district level, I knew how important but also how risky it was for me to navigate the cultural and political differences in the district. I knew I had to garner support from allies and address the concerns of detractors whether they were staff members, elected officials, or policy makers to ensure quality programs for English learners. This was risky business for a young Latina professional such as me. But something deep inside me bolstered my confidence. The values and beliefs passed to me by strong and proud family members who cared for me deeply and expected great things from me, strengthened my resolve to make a life-changing difference in the lives of bicultural/bilingual students. At this time, I realized the importance of not only having professional mentors such as Momoyo but also strong cultural mentors who were bold in their advocacy, in spite of the costs and criticism.

Emerging Awareness of Cultural Barriers

When I returned to the classroom, I was asked to take on the assignment of Child Welfare and Attendance Supervisor (CWA). I learned another part of the school that I had only observed from the perspective of a classroom teacher. Here, I worked with counselors, teachers, parents, and the entire administrative team to improve the attendance of students. Once again, I observed firsthand how opportunities and resources were inequitably distributed and accessed by *all* students. Most at risk were the ESL students. With so much evidence to me of the barriers and impediments to school attendance, engagement, and success for ESL students, my advocacy was reinforced, and I became very protective of our ESL students, worrying about them when they would go the high school.

Mary Gonzalez Mend, Mentor

After I served a year as the CWA supervisor, I returned to the classroom. That year, we had a new district bilingual coordinator, Dr. Mary Gonzales Mend. Dr. Mend had been the first Latina principal in Montebello Unified School District. When Dr. Mend asked me to take on the assignment of professional development services member, a teacher on special assignment, I was excited about the opportunity, much to the protestation of my principal! Dr. Mend was eventually able to get me released, and I served two years with Dr. Mend, where I learned so much. I had never worked for a woman supervisor before, and felt so fortunate to learn from her and from other women on the team who remain good friends and colleagues to this day. It was during this tenure that I gained full awareness of my culture and my gender as strengths of leadership. I knew the challenges to the successful leadership journeys of so many women like me, and realized that I had a responsibility as a trailblazer and as sister to mentor them, so that they, too, could embrace their gender and culture, related wisdom, knowledge, and disposition.

Bilingual Coordinator, First Administrator Position

Dr. Mend decided to leave the district in 1980; at the same time, I would be returning to Montebello Intermediate School. I decided to apply for the position of coordinator of bilingual/bicultural education, and was hired in July 1980.

Being a young administrator and a female in a district dominated by males was a good test of my strengths and values. Bilingual education was not embraced by everyone, even though MUSD was known for its outstanding bilingual programs and staff. We still had many in influential positions on the board and at the administrative level that opposed any directives or policies on bilingual education in general, and challenge me personally. What I learned from this experience is that it is not enough to stand firm in my beliefs. I also had to influence the opinions of other important decision makers and always anticipate criticism to respond in a proactive stance.

Aspiring to Principal Role: First Principalship

I had always believed that principals were the key to student success, and during the first year as the new bilingual/bicultural coordinator, my belief was confirmed; principals are the key administrative position in a district. As I worked with principals in my new position, I saw that they were the gatekeepers for the success of any instructional program. They determined who was sent to training, how money was allocated, which staff members were supported, and which, if any, new instructional program would be implemented. I then begin thinking of becoming a principal.

In July of 1981, I was appointed principal of Washington Elementary School where I spent four years learning through trial and error, but learning many leadership skills and humbling life lessons, nonetheless. First and foremost, I learned you must move your staff from where they are, not where you think they are or where you think they should be. These hard lessons were learned while being nurtured and mentored by the best. All of them taught me about leadership, risk, trust, and integrity. But most of all, they taught me to hold on to your core beliefs and values despite the challenges. And for me, this had come to mean to embrace the parts of my identity from which those core values emanated: my identity as daughter, sister, mother, wife, and my proud stalwart cultural heritage.

Principal of an Intermediate School

In 1987, I was appointed principal of Montebello Intermediate School, the school where I began my teaching career. It was such an honor. Many of the same teachers who were there when I started were still there. It was still an amazing school. At the same time I started at Montebello Intermediate School, I began my doctoral studies at USC. Attending USC was an exceptional professional and personal experience. Amazingly, there were several other Latinas in the program. Nevertheless, it was a very intense time for me. I was going to school and doing my best to balance work with family. As a Latina, the family responsibilities are paramount, but I was on a mission with my professional goals and aspirations. My quest for educational equity for bilingual/bicultural students was born from personal and cultural experiences, and reinforced by my professional experiences, they were driving me. I began to realize that I was operating both in my personal life and in my professional life from the same moral imperative: to do all I could do to make a difference in people's lives where it mattered most. What I have learned is that the work is hard, but necessary, and one must have a strong network of family and friends to succeed.

Leadership Opportunities

While principal at Montebello Intermediate, on October 1, 1987, the Whittier earthquake jolted our community. With a magnitude of more than 5.5, our school experienced the most damage in the area. Our main building suffered structural damage, and we were unable to house 900 students of our 1,800 students. This was before cell phones, faxes, e-mails, and all the technology we have today. The daunting task of keeping our staff and community notified was paramount. All communication was done via U.S. mail and personal calls.

    This emergency tested all of my leadership skills. First, I realized I had a tremendous administrative team and an amazing staff. But I had to make several key decisions that would impact all of them.

My first decision was to require all my staff to report to work the next three days at 8:30 a.m. for an update on the status of the building and when we would reopen. We only had three days to plan for the reopening of school before the weekend and resuming school on Monday. A few staff were upset about having to return the next day, but to my surprise, when they returned, they all seemed to be in good spirits and happy to see one another. I shared with the staff that we could not occupy the main building for several weeks and possibly months. The main building had suffered severe structural damage. The staff was open to discussing all options, and they were more than happy to come in every day to get updates. Besides the updates, the staff found time to take care of one another. As expected, several staff members also suffered earthquake damage at their homes. Many staff members spent the day counseling, listening to, and showing deep care for one another. This strong mutual support helped many through the process of recovery.

At the end of the three days, we determined we needed to go to double sessions for several months. The second decision I had to make was determining which staff would be in the morning and afternoon sessions. Again, the staff came together and helped with the master schedule. In fact, it was clear who preferred the morning or afternoon session. These natural biological clocks came in handy when determining the staff schedule. Just as our students, some of our teachers preferred starting early and others starting later.

We learned a lot about ourselves as a staff. The Chinese define crisis as *opportunity*. And all of us took this crisis as an opportunity for personal and professional growth. Despite the incredible disruptions, we continued to provide professional development and made incredible progress to improving our curriculum. To this day, many from Montebello Intermediate who were there during this time call it the "Camelot" days. The staff came together to support one another, as well as the students, the parents, and the entire community. We got to know one another in so many different ways. We learned so much more about one another's strengths and vulnerability, but more important, we learned to support one another in new and exciting ways. We found we could trust one another, and we gained so much from one another each and every day. Silos were broken down, and we were a "professional learning community" before this term was popular. It was an exciting and inspirational time, one where I personally and professionally learned so many lessons. I learned that during a crisis be prepared to involve everyone because they want to contribute. And as a leader, it is not your decision how an individual will contribute, but it is up to you to allow and accept the contribution in any form it comes. It just may not be what you expect as the leader, but accept it and be grateful. As the leader, you must be open and transparent with all your communication, to keep everyone informed.

The Assistant Superintendency— New Opportunities

During and after the earthquake, I learned many things. I learned that during a crisis, and for women in particular and more so for women of color, you are in a fishbowl, and everyone is observing your actions and your words. During a crisis, the questions on everyone's mind are how you handle the crisis, can they depend on you, and do people look to you as the leader. During the crisis, I was so immersed in the work, I had not paid attention to others reaction. I learned a few valuable life lessons early on. As a woman, and a Latina, you are always going to be observed to see if you can handle the challenges presented to you. But I also learned that you personally don't have to take the credit, you must give your staff public recognition for work well done and make sure those around you help others be their best, at a school or at the district office.

The following year, I was asked by the superintendent to take a position as acting assistant superintendent of pupil and support services. This was interesting since this was the division responsible for emergency preparedness. Prior to this time, I had no inclination or desire to take on an administrative position at the district office. I loved being a principal, especially at Montebello Intermediate. I decided to take the risk and accepted the offer to become the acting assistant superintendent. To this day, I wonder how much my performance during and after the earthquake influenced the perception of policy makers who offered me the position of assistant superintendent.

I began my new position as acting assistant superintendent in September of 1988. I was the first and only female assistant superintendent for the district, again another first. At the time, I was also the only Latino on the superintendent's cabinet. One big advantage I had taking on this new assignment was the support from my colleagues. I recall a visit from one of my colleagues on cabinet. He shared an important lesson that I have never forgotten: "Darline, when the problems come to you, all the easy answers are gone. They are now coming to you for your help to solve the problems that could not be solved earlier or at a lower level." As I moved into administration, this statement has proven to be so true. I have kept that statement at heart, and try to get problems and issues resolved at the local level as much as possible.

After a few months as acting assistant superintendent, I was named the permanent assistant superintendent. I enjoyed this position very much because I was responsible for many new initiatives: drop-out prevention programs that piloted several progressive programs and reduced the drop-out numbers; implemented a behavioral health program as part of lawsuit settlement caused by a suicide attempt at one of our schools; provided new guidelines for identification of gifted students focused on English learner and Latino students; and created and implemented the first districtwide parent conference, to name a few of the initiatives.

Superintendent: Challenges and New Experiences

In December 1990, during the holiday break, our superintendent called his cabinet into his office and told us the district was bankrupt! We were all stunned. In the late 1980s, we had heard from the new business manager that we would be facing difficult times and that we were spending our reserves on ongoing expenses that would eventually get MUSD into financial difficulty. In January 1991, the superintendent informed the board and the staff about the impending bankruptcy. If the district did not take appropriate action to become fiscally solvent, which, by law, required a state loan, the state would assign a state trustee that would take over all responsibilities and make all fiscal and personnel decisions of the district. By the end of the year, the superintendent and the business manager decided to retire. I learned critical lessons during this budget crisis. First, how critical it is to have a good staff; second, to have accurate budget numbers; and then communicate to the all stakeholders on a regular basis all the details of the situation. The staff wants to know their leaders have the information they need to make good decisions, and they want to be involved and informed.

In late June 1991, the board decided to interview a few cabinet members for the position of an interim superintendent. I was one of the cabinet members who was interviewed, and at the time, I did not know if I could do the job. But after the interview, I believed I could return the district to fiscal solvency and continue the great programs for our students.

I began as the interim superintendent on July 1, 1991. The board gave me two goals: We would be fiscally solvent, and we would continue to make academic progress. It was a very sobering feeling to know that I was now responsible for ensuring the fiscal health of the third largest district in the state. But despite all the apprehension and nerves, I believed I was capable of doing the job.

My first major responsibility was to hire a new business manager. I knew this was critical if Montebello was going to become fiscally solvent over time. And I also knew what could happen if I hired the wrong person. I decided to hire from within, and the board appointed Mr. Glen Sheppard. But both Glen and I never acted as if were interim or acting. We had a job to do. We made a commitment to do whatever necessary to bring the district to fiscal solvency. Immediately, I had to learn about district budgets and state finances. It was a steep learning curve. I learned all I could about budgets, reserves, trends, state funding, and state finances. Glen was a wonderful teacher.

As the budget committee began to make a list of recommended cuts to programs, it was clear that the cuts alone would not balance our budget. To balance our budget, we would have to ask for salary reductions as well. We held many public meetings to discuss proposed cuts. Hundreds of community members, students, and teachers attended.

I recall several events that describe the atmosphere in the district at the time. The board had many proposals to review, and one recommended the reduction and the possible elimination of some of the high school sports programs. Once the high school staff and students heard this, we had three days of student walkouts. One day, the students turned into an angry mob, and the local police had to come in riot gear to stop students from breaking storefront windows and causing other personal and property damage. Fortunately, none of our students were hurt during the three-day walkouts, and the board did not eliminate the sports program.

We also continued with the districtwide budget committee. The committee made many recommendations to the board that I call "the low-hanging fruit." When it got to the point where the committee had to actually recommend cutting key staff and programs, they decided they would stop meeting and asked me to make the final recommendations to the board.

As I sat one night in my office creating my final list of cuts, I looked over to my executive assistant and I said to her, "I now know how a general must feel." As I sat there and developed my list of cuts, I thought of it as a general going to war. He is developing a battle plan, knowing there will be casualties. His primary goal and responsibility is to minimize the casualties, but he absolutely knows there will be losses. As I reflected on my plan, I was doing the same. I looked at my list, I knew the people on the list, and I knew their work, and I knew there would be major losses for students and staff and casualties to many successful programs for our students. Just like a general, my responsibility was to minimize those casualties, and I began to cry! It was one of the most difficult decisions I have ever had to make in my career. As an educator, you choose this profession to make a difference in students' lives and to give them the best education possible. And for many young people, education is their lifeline and hope to a better future. And in an instant, those opportunities are reduced or eliminated, and there is no way to regain the losses in a short time. The adults, on the other hand, get the time to wait for budgets to improve, and sometimes do this again and again, just as we are doing now in our current recession. But a third grader only gets to do third grade once. Our students only have a short window of opportunity to get this right.

The good news is that within two years, we achieved our goal, and we were fiscally solvent. We never had to go to the state for a loan. This was the combined effort of the board's commitment to make the tough decisions, staff also conceding to a salary cut, and the community understanding the tough sacrifices everyone had to make to remain an independent district, without a state trustee.

But despite these very difficult times, our district still managed to focus on students. For the first time in many years, the district created a strategic plan and a vision statement. We invited all stakeholders and representatives from every school to attend the planning meetings. Even though we were going through very difficult times, we all made a commitment to work together on behalf of the students.

Ethical Decisions

As I continued to work during these difficult times, I was also aware that things could change at any time. We had a board election, and new board members were elected. As expected, the community blamed many of the board members for the financial crisis. The new board members believed they could do it better and would be more involved in the day-to-day operations of the district.

In February of 1992, the board hired me as the permanent superintendent. I succeeded in meeting the demands of the job, and met the two goals set by the board. Within two years, we were fiscally solvent, and we were making progress on the academic side.

In May of 1994, I had my first personnel problem with the new board. The district had a process for the selection and hiring new principals. After several interviews, the final three to five candidates were sent to the superintendent for a final interview and then a recommendation to the board. I was following the process when I received a call from a board member indicating the he and two others had a candidate they wanted me to recommend. I was stunned. First, this had never happened before. And second, the person they wanted me to recommend had not placed in the top five in any of the interview panels. When I objected, he told me that he and another board member had made this commitment to this person as part of campaign promises. Not only stunned, now in complete disbelief, I was speechless.

I just could not accept that this was happening. I asked myself over and over again, does this happen to all superintendents? Am I just being picky or naïve? I then decided to call my mentor, Dr. Mary Mend. She agreed with me that this was wrong, and reassured me this isn't the way it should be done. Mary then suggested I call superintendent Ray Cortines and ask his advice. At that time, Ray was the chancellor of New York City Schools. I called and left a message, and he immediately called me back. I will always thank Ray for taking the time to call me. I did not know Ray, but his call to me told me a lot about Ray as a person. Ray always finds time to mentor and assist superintendents and others, even if he doesn't know the person. I told him the story and he responded in a few words, "The only thing a superintendent has is his or her integrity."

I spoke to the board, and I told them I could not make this recommendation, and that if they chose to move forward with the appointment, I would only stay for the remainder of my contract and then leave. I knew I was right in taking a stand against the board's directive. If I let this happen, I could not remain in the district. I never thought of leaving Montebello, my home and the district that I had grown up in and loved dearly. But I knew if the board did this, I could not live with it. The majority of the board insisted on this action, and I knew I had to leave.

At a board meeting, I took the board action to the board, but I was very clear in the motion, that it was the board making the recommendation not the superintendent. I refused to put my name on the recommendation.

Time to Leave the Nest

During summer, while I was dealing with the personnel problem, I had been receiving calls from a search firm asking me if I was interested in the position of superintendent in Salt Lake City School District (SLCSD). I declined several times because, at that time, I still had hope the board members would take my original recommendation. Once the board took the action in August, I realized that I now needed to look outside and find another job. There were several openings in southern California. But I decided that if I was going to make a move, I should make a *big move*! I called the search firm handling the SLCSD search and asked if it was still open. They told me it had closed, but in reality, it was open until filled. I told them I was interested. After several interviews, I received a call, and the head of the search committee told me that I was in the finals, and they wanted me to meet with the board! I was absolutely stunned. It was time now to take this seriously. If I got the job, I was going to have to move—alone—to Salt Lake City, where I didn't know a soul and begin all over.

I met with the board of Salt Lake City School District the following weekend, and had a wonderful interview. I instantly felt very comfortable with the board and was very impressed with the student board member.

A few days after the board met with me, I was informed that I was one of three finalists, and it was going to be made public. I would be invited back to meet with community and other stakeholders before a final decision would be made.

It was now time to tell the board in Montebello. I met with the board in Montebello the next week, and told them I was a finalist in SLC.

The following week, I met with the Salt Lake City community and all stakeholders for an entire day. At the end of the day, I met with the SLC board. The week of September 24, I was notified that I had been selected, and the Salt Lake School board wanted to make a site visit to meet with the Montebello board, staff, parents, and community. The meeting took place the first week in October. By that time, the community was aware that I might be leaving; they were very upset. I never stated why I was leaving; a few people knew, but I did not want to make the reason public. There were still too many scars and so much emotion from the budget crisis that I didn't want to cause more emotional upheaval. I just stated publicly this was a great opportunity for me.

I left Montebello in December 1994, and began my new position in Salt Lake City School District in January 1995. And I never looked back.

Superintendent as CEO/Capital City, Capital Gains of 'Olympic' Proportions

I arrived in Salt Lake City in January 1995. One board member from SLC said the board hired me because of my successful leadership experience in Montebello, including my work with curriculum and instruction, community involvement, and experience with a diverse population; and the fact that I was Latina was a plus.

I immediately began immersing myself in the school and community culture. I knew I had been successful in Montebello, but I had no history with the community in SLC. I had to gain the trust of the community, and they also had to get to know me. I spent my first three months meeting with different school groups and community organizations.

Immediately upon arriving, I had to deal with problems that needed to be resolved. But I knew that I could not solve them without first understanding the context in which the problems existed. My tenure in Salt Lake was filled with what I called "blips." Our focus was on improving student achievement, reducing the drop-out rate, and increasing the college-going rate of students in all student subgroups. But as in any organization, some events will take you away from the focus—if you allow the "blip" to take over the days and weeks it takes to solve these issues. I have summarized a few of the key blips:

- *Religion in the curriculum.* When I arrived in January of 1995, I met with a parent who alleged a choir teacher was proselytizing and requiring his daughter to attend "fire chats" on field trips and only singing hymns from the dominant religion. This situation came to a head in the spring when the parent filed a lawsuit suing the district and the teacher. The parent also filed for an injunction on the day of graduation ordering the district not to allow a religious hymn to be sung at graduation. As expected, the students broke out in song, and we ended up in federal court for several years. The case went to the U.S. Supreme Court, who declined to hear the case and let the 10th Circuit opinion stand in favor of the district.
- *Gay Straight Alliance.* In the fall of 1995, our assistant superintendent for high schools received a question from the principal

of East High School about the formation of a Gay Straight Alliance club. The first thing I asked was to see the policy on equal access. To my surprise, the district did not have a policy. In absence of a policy, it was my opinion the Gay Straight Alliance club could be formed. This opinion was not readily accepted by some on the board or in the community. The board discussed the issue for several months before making a decision on a new policy. In late spring of the following school year, the board voted to ban all extracurricular clubs on a four to three vote. It was now up to me and my staff to make this new policy work for the students. We began by providing the community with opportunities to come together to support the Gay Straight Alliance in Salt Lake City. But despite all our good efforts, there was still tension at the high schools with students blaming students for the loss of their extracurricular clubs. The tension got so bad I had to ask for outside help. I began by being direct with the community about the negative behavior of some students and community members toward the students in the Gay Straight Alliance. A few good friends advised me to go the Latter Day Saints First Presidency. Through their contacts, I was able to meet with President Hinckley and the First Presidency, and I asked for their advice. President Hinckley was very supportive of my goal to ensure student safety, and he assigned a church leader to work with me over the next several months. Over time, the tension subsided. After three years, the Board changed the board policy and allowed extracurricular clubs to exist.

- *Equity issues/Annenberg grant:* When I arrived in SLC, the city was experiencing many demographic changes: an increase in the number of English learners, more students from different ethnic groups, and more students living in poverty. My goal was to make this data transparent. If we did not share this data, our public would not be able to understand the challenges in our schools. We began to disaggregate data by all subgroups. I also had to confront a state data system that did not include English learners in the system. To implement a reform agenda, we decided to apply for funds from the Annenberg Foundation. We were pleased to be awarded a $12 million grant. This was the impetus to make major changes in our programs to meet the diverse needs of our students. Over time, our public began to understand the term "equity" as it pertained to our students. The grant energized the district and the community. We began to look at data and become transparent about our work, and we all focused on becoming culturally proficient. Teachers were the core of the reform and had a vote on all the key reform agenda. Over time, our test scores continued to increase and our drop-out rate decreased. The focus on the three-day district-wide professional development for six years was on cultural proficiency and English learners.

- *Bond/new schools:* As is my practice, I visited every school in the district my first six months on the job. In my visits, I noticed that on the west side of the district classrooms were in the cafeteria and on the stage or in small trailers. While on the east side, the most affluent part of the district, there were extra classrooms and teachers had plenty of space, even teacher lounges, that didn't exist in some of the schools on the west side. I immediately made a decision to change this, and within a short amount of time, I had new trailers at the schools that needed the space. The board agreed with my decision. The district had previously had a bond approved by the voters to retrofit the schools to withstand earthquakes. By 1996, most of the bond money had been spent on the four high schools. We decided to ask the voters to approve a new bond to build new elementary schools on the west side to meet the growing population—replace older schools and upgrade others. The bond passed with more than 73% approval.

  I left SLCSD with more than 12 new schools on the west side. The students, teachers, and the community felt valued and appreciated. For me, this was an equity issue. We began the new building program on the west side to make sure students who had been ignored for too long were now getting the attention and respect they deserved.

- *School closures:* As the demographics shifted and budgets got tight the board began to discuss school closures. The community was opposed to school closures, even with the data that clearly demonstrated we had too many schools with small student enrollment. It is never easy to close a school, but it had to be done if we were going to maximize our resources.

As mentioned early, the previous events I referred to as "blips" because we still had to focus on teaching and learning and improving student achievement.

My last year, I had one final blip: planning for the 2002 Winter Olympics. Prior to September 11, 2001, everyone in the city and school district were excited about "welcoming the world to our city." In Salt Lake City, our student demographics represented the world, so we were thrilled to be part of the once-in-lifetime experience. The board made the decision to keep schools open during the Olympics so students would have a structured learning experience and also be transported to several Olympic events. This decision was not without controversy. Staff wanted to be off so they could volunteer and be part of the games. Parents with the resources to purchase tickets did not want their child missing the Olympics and lobbied the board to close school during the Olympics. But the board held firm. After September 11, 2001, staff and community at several schools that were close to the downtown Olympic venues worried about their security and demanded the board close their schools during the Olympics. The staff and community were not concerned how the time would be made up. After much deliberation, the board conceded, and allowed three schools to close during the Olympics. As we all know, the Salt Lake City Olympics were a success! I was fortunate to have been personally involved in many different ways. I worked with the Olympic committee to ensure that students in Utah were given free tickets to attend many of the events; many of our students participated in the opening and closing ceremonies, both for the Olympics and the Special Olympics. I was mayor for the day at the Olympic Village, and also participated in the opening and closing ceremonies by carrying the flag for Croatia.

Throughout my eight years in Salt Lake City, I learned many lessons. I learned when you focus on your mission—student learning—you get results! And when you get results, you can deal with the blips. I also learned that I had to take a stand on issues that were not popular with the majority—but as a leader you must or you sell yourself short, but you also hurt students if you don't. I also learned through this experience how to work with the media. And one important lesson I learned over and over again: never be afraid to ask for help!

Superintendent as Public Servant

In the summer of 2001, the position of superintendent for the Los Angeles County Office of Education (LACOE) was advertised. I was encouraged by many colleagues in Los Angeles to apply. I had the final interview and was offered the job as superintendent of LACOE on June 23, 2002. In Los Angeles County, the county superintendent is hired by the Los Angeles County board of supervisors, yet works directly with an appointed board of education

When I arrived in September, the first thing I heard from some top management was that I got the job because I was Mexican, not because I had the experience. It is just a reminder, no matter our (i.e., qualified Latinas) experience, our credentials (PhD), our good reputation, our successes—some will believe we got it because of our color and gender!

The eight years as the superintendent of LACOE were some of the best I have had in my career. I will always cherish the opportunity to work with 80 superintendents in the largest regional educational center in the country. My staff and I were very privileged to be part of such a diverse organization that influences the lives of more than 2.25 million children.

When I took on the superintendency, LACOE had an overall negative reputation with our school districts, even though some individuals were highly regarded by district staff. Departments in the same organization worked in isolation and in silos. There was much duplication of services and responsibilities. I began to work on changing organizational culture and the reputation we had with our public. Doing this in a larger organization is not easy to do. My first priority was to develop a good working relationship with my staff and the district superintendents by reaching out to both of them to assess their needs. The priority of my new strategic plan was focused on effective customer service and effective use of personal and fiscal resources.

As in Salt Lake, I spent my first three to four months meeting with each assistant superintendent, directors, union leaders, principals, board of education, superintendents, and board of supervisors offices to learn about the programs, their concerns, their successes, and what they liked about working at or with LACOE. As I learned in SLCSD, it is important for a leader to learn about an organization's culture directly from the people who work in the organization as well as those who are their customers. A leader cannot make decisions until information and data is collected authentically.

An important lesson that I learned at LACOE was the importance of making the goal of customer service intentional. Making a goal intentional is infusing it to the day-to-day operations of all employees. For example, all managers were required to include in their performance evaluations a specific plan for improving customer relations for their particular product and/or service. This required every employee to be accountable for improving customer service. Remember, organizations are only as good as the individual employees. When individuals take on personal responsibility for customer service, the entire organization succeeds.

The goal of quality customer service requires the service providers have knowledge of their customers' background, experience, cultures, and their wants and their needs from the perspective of the customer not the service provider. This required ongoing professional development across all departments for all employees to exam their behaviors, attitudes, and actions to develop culturally competent behaviors, practices, and beliefs about their diverse clientele.

I also created the opportunity to forge a common vision of advocacy for underserved communities by coalescing the voices of 80 superintendents into a common commitment to educational equity. I did this by promoting a culture of learning, teaching, and leading by providing ongoing professional development for the superintendents.

This experience at LACOE allowed me to see that education is a microcosm of society. Our role as educators is to facilitate and create this continued conversation on behalf of all students. The opportunity I had to lead an organization such as LACOE allowed me to focus every day on the big picture: the importance of education to improve the lives of all students to be successful, and to live, contribute, and actively participate in a democratic society.

New Journey

I retired from LACOE in August 2010 to take a position with the University of Southern California. I was hired as a clinical professor to create and implement a new master's degree program for school leaders. Early in my career, I realized the importance of having a great principal lead a school and personally observed many outstanding principals. I now have the opportunity to make a difference in this area, and I hope influence the lives of many, many students.

Resource F

Cultural Proficiency Books Matrix

How to Use Our Books

Book	Authors	Focus
Cultural Proficiency: A Manual for School Leaders, 3rd ed., 2009	Randall B. Lindsey Kikanza Nuri Robins Raymond D. Terrell	This book is an introduction to cultural proficiency. There is extended discussion of each of the tools and the historic framework for diversity work.
Culturally Proficient Instruction: A Guide for People Who Teach, 2nd ed., 2005	Kikanza Nuri Robins Randall B. Lindsey Delores B. Lindsey Raymond D. Terrell	This book focuses on the five essential elements and can be directed to anyone in an instructional role. This book can be used as a workbook for a study group.
The Culturally Proficient School: An Implementation Guide for School Leaders, 2005	Randall B. Lindsey Laraine M. Roberts Franklin CampbellJones	This book guides the reader to examine their school as a cultural organization and to design and implement approaches to dialogue and inquiry.
Culturally Proficient Coaching: Supporting Educators to Create Equitable Schools, 2007	Delores B. Lindsey Richard S. Martinez Randall B. Lindsey	This book aligns the essential elements with Costa and Garmston's Cognitive Coaching model. The book provides coaches, teachers, and administrators a personal guidebook with protocols and maps for conducting conversations that shift thinking in support of all students achieving at levels higher than ever before.

(Continued)

(Continued)

Book	Authors	Focus
Culturally Proficient Inquiry: A Lens for Identifying and Examining Educational Gaps, 2008	Randall B. Lindsey Stephanie M. Graham R. Chris Westphal, Jr. Cynthia L. Jew	This book uses protocols for gathering and analyzing student achievement and access data as well as rubrics for gathering and analyzing data about educator practices. A CD accompanies the book for easy downloading and use of the data protocols.
Culturally Proficient Leadership: The Personal Journey Begins Within, 2009	Raymond D. Terrell Randall B. Lindsey	This book guides the reader through the development of a cultural autobiography as a means to becoming an increasingly effective leader in our diverse society.
Culturally Proficient Learning Communities: Confronting Inequities Through Collaborative Curiosity, 2009	Delores B. Lindsey Linda D. Jungwirth Jarvis V.N.C. Pahl Randall B. Lindsey	This book provides readers a lens through which to examine the purpose, the intentions, and the progress of learning communities to which they belong or wish to develop. School and district leaders are provided protocols, activities, and rubrics to engage in actions focused on the intersection of race, ethnicity, gender, social-class, sexual orientation and identity, faith, and ableness with the disparities in student achievement.
The Cultural Proficiency Journey: Moving Beyond Ethical Barriers Toward Profound School Change, 2010	Franklin CampbellJones Brenda CampbellJones Randall B. Lindsey	This book explores cultural proficiency as an ethical construct. It makes transparent the connection between values, assumptions, beliefs, and observable behavior making change possible and sustainable.
Culturally Proficient Education: An Assets-Based Response to Conditions of Poverty, 2010	Randall B. Lindsey Michelle S. Karns Keith Myatt	This book is designed for educators to learn how to identify and develop the strengths of students from low-income backgrounds.
Culturally Proficient Collaboration: Use and Misuse of School Counselors, 2011	Diana L. Stephens Randall B. Lindsey	This book uses the lens of Cultural Proficiency to frame the American Association of School Counselor's performance standards and Education Trust's Transforming School Counseling Initiative as means for addressing issues of access and equity in schools in collaborative school leadership teams.

Book	Authors	Focus
A Culturally Proficient Society Begins in School: Leadership for Equity, 2011	Carmella S. Franco Maria G. Ott Darline P. Robles	This book frames the life stories of three superintendents through the lens of Cultural Proficiency. The reader is provided the opportunity to design or modify his or her leadership for equity plan.
Culturally Proficient Organizations: A Conversation with Colleagues about the Practice of Cultural Proficiency (working title), Expected 2012	Kikanza Nuri Robins Delores B. Lindsey	This book answers the question, How do you do it? It is directed to managers and organizational leaders who want to introduce cultural proficiency systemically.

References

American Civil Liberties Union (ACLU) of Southern California. (2007, August). *Williams vs. California: The statewide impact of two years of implementation.* Los Angeles, CA: ACLU.

Anderson, Peggy. (2007). *Great quotes from great leaders.* Naperville, IL: Simple Truths.

Barker, Joel. (Producer). (1996). *Paradigm principles.* [DVD]. Burnsville, MN: Charthouse International Learning Corporation.

Bass, Bernard M., & Riggio, Ronald E. (2006). *Transformational leadership.* (2nd ed.), Mahwah, NJ: Lawrence Erlbaum.

CampbellJones, Franklin, CampbellJones, Brenda, & Lindsey, Randall B. (2010). *The cultural proficiency journey: Moving beyond ethical barriers toward profound school change.* Thousand Oaks, CA: Corwin.

Conners, Dennis Arthur, & Poutiatine, Michael. (2010). Transformational learning for school leaders: Movement for social justice in school leader preparation. Retrieved from http://cnx.org/content/m34883/1.3/

Cross, Terry L., Bazron, Barbara J., Dennis, Karl W., & Isaacs, Mareasa R. (1989). *Toward a culturally competent system of care, Volume 1.* Washington, DC: Georgetown University Child Development Program, Child and Adolescent Service System Program.

Freire, Paulo. (1987). *Pedagogy of the oppressed.* New York, NY: Continuum.

Fullan, Michael. (2003). *The moral imperative of school leadership.* Thousand Oaks, CA: Corwin.

Fullan, Michael. (2010). *All systems go: The change imperative for whole system reform.* Thousand Oaks, CA: Corwin.

Glass, Thomas E., & Franceschini, Louis, A. (2007). *The state of the American school superintendency: A mid-decade report.* Latham, MD: Rowman & Littlefield Education.

Grogan, Margaret, & Shakeshaft, Charol. (2011). *Women and educational leadership.* San Francisco, CA: Jossey-Bass.

Hirsch, Jr., Eric D. (1987). *Cultural literacy: What every American needs to know.* Boston, MA: Houghton Mifflin.

Kowalski, Theodore J., McCord, Robert S., Petersen, George J., Young, I. Philip, & Ellerson, Noelle M. (2011). *The American school superintendent: 2010 decennial study.* Lanham, MD: Rowman & Littlefield Education.

Lindsey, Delores B., Jungwirth, Linda D., Pahl, Jarvis V.N.V., & Lindsey, Randall B. *Culturally proficient learning communities: Confronting inequities through collaborative curiosity.* Thousand Oaks, CA: Corwin.

Lindsey, Delores B., Martinez, Richard S., & Lindsey, Randall B. (2007). *Culturally proficient coaching: Supporting educators to create equitable schools.* Thousand Oaks, CA: Corwin.

Lindsey, Randall B., Graham, Stephanie M., Westphal, Jr., Chris R., & Jew, Cynthia L. (2008). *Culturally proficient inquiry: A lens for identifying and examining educational gaps.* Thousand Oaks, CA: Corwin.

Lindsey, Randall B., Karns, Michelle, S., & Myatt, Keith. (2010). *Culturally proficient education: An assets-based response to conditions of poverty.* Thousand Oaks, CA: Corwin.

Lindsey, Randall B., Nuri Robins, Kikanza, & Terrell, Raymond D. (1999). *Cultural proficiency: A manual for school leaders.* Thousand Oaks, CA: Corwin.

Lindsey, Randall B., Nuri Robins, Kikanza, & Terrell, Raymond D. (2003). *Cultural proficiency: A manual for school leaders,* (3rd ed.). Thousand Oaks, CA: Corwin.

Lindsey, Randall B., Nuri Robins, Kikanza, & Terrell, Raymond D. (2009). *Cultural proficiency: A manual for school leaders* (3rd ed.). Thousand Oaks, CA: Corwin.

Lindsey, Randall B., Roberts, Laraine M., & CampbellJones, Franklin. (2005). *The culturally proficient school: An implementation guide for school leaders.* Thousand Oaks, CA: Corwin.

Meléndez de Santa Ana, Thelma. (2008, September/October). So you want to be a superintendent? *Leadership.* 37(7), 24–27. Sacramento, CA: Association of California School Administrators.

Moll, Luis C. (2010). Mobilizing culture, language and educational practices: Fulfilling the promises of *Mendez* and *Brown. Educational Researcher,* 39(6), 451–460.

National Center for Education Statistics. (2007). *Schools and staffing survey (SASS): A brief profile of America's public schools.* Washington, DC: U.S. Department of Education.

Nuri Robins, Kikanza, Lindsey, Randall B., Lindsey, Delores B., & Terrell, Raymond D. (2002). *Culturally proficient instruction: A guide for people who teach.* Thousand Oaks, CA: Corwin.

Palmer, Parker J. (2000). *Let your life speak: Listening for the voice of vocation.* San Francisco, CA: Jossey-Bass.

Perie, Marianne, Moran, Rebecca, & Lutkus, Anthony D. (2005). *NAEP 2004 trends in academic progress: Three decades of student performance in reading and mathematics* (NCES 2005–464). Washington, DC: U.S. Department of Education.

Ravitch, Diane. (2010). *The death and life of the great American school system: How testing and choice are undermining education.* New York, NY: Basic Books.

Senge, Peter M., Cambron-McCabe, Nelda H., Lucas, Timothy, Kleiner, Art, Dutton, Janis, et al. (Eds.). (2000). *Schools that learn: A fifth discipline fieldbook for educators, parents, and everyone who cares about education.* New York, NY: Doubleday.

Snyder, Thomas D., Dillow, Sally A., & Hoffman, Charlene M. (2009). *Digest of education statistics 2008* (NCES 2009–020). Washington, DC: National Center for Education Statistics.

Stephens, Diana L., & Lindsey, Randall B. (2011). *Culturally proficient collaboration: Use and misuse of school counselors.* Thousand Oaks, CA: Corwin.

Terrell, Raymond D., & Lindsey, Randall B. (2009). *Culturally proficient leadership: The personal journey begins within.* Thousand Oaks, CA: Corwin.

U.S. Department of Education. (2007). *A brief profile of America's public schools.* Washington, DC: Author.

Index